Bluebird China

Kenna and Bob Rosen

Schiffer Publishing Ltd ®

4880 Lower Valley Road, Atglen, PA 19310 USA

Dedication

This book is dedicated to our bluebirds, Woody and Mackie.

Designed by Joseph M. Riggio Jr.
Type set in University Roman Bd BT/Korinna BT

ISBN: 0-7643-1864-0
Printed in China
1 2 3 4

Published by Schiffer Publishing Ltd.
4880 Lower Valley Road
Atglen, PA 19310
Phone: (610) 593-1777; Fax: (610) 593-2002
E-mail: Info@schifferbooks.com
Please visit our web site catalog at **www.schifferbooks.com**
We are always looking for people to write books on new and
related subjects. If you have an idea for a book, please
contact us at the above address.

This book may be purchased from the publisher.
Include $3.95 for shipping.
Please try your bookstore first.
You may write for a free catalog.

In Europe, Schiffer books are distributed by
Bushwood Books
6 Marksbury Avenue
Kew Gardens
Surrey TW9 4JF England
Phone: 44 (0) 20 8392 8585
Fax: 44 (0) 20 8392 9876
E-mail: Bushwd@aol.com
Free postage in the UK. Europe: air mail at cost.

Contents

Acknowledgments

This book is the result of a trip down a very long and winding road. We must first thank our children for enduring countless stops at the antique malls and shops along this road as well as the time we took from them in the actual writing and photographing of the book.

We are very grateful for the kind assistance of the Museum of Ceramics, East Liverpool, Ohio, in giving us access to their archives and in particular, Anastasia Sfakis. Additionally, Linda Kennedy of the Buffalo Erie County Historical Society, Buffalo, New York, was very generous with her time and help.

Much thanks to Stephanie and Tom Trambaugh, Patti Mainard-Miller, Joan Sloat of the Now and Then Shoppe, Fort Smith, Arkansas, and Susan Wright for graciously allowing us to photograph their bluebird china.

A very big thank you goes to Larry Fleming and Sharon Mitchell for their expert photographic consultation.

Thank you to Dorrie Russell Sacksteder for information on W. S. George Pottery Company and Janice Lane for information on Albright China Company.

Last, thanks to all the bluebird fans everywhere, especially Melody Byard. This book would not have been possible without your comments and encouragement.

Introduction

The incredible popularity of bluebird china in the 1920s could properly have been characterized as a "craze." And like many "crazes" viewed from the perspective of several decades away, it may be hard to understand. Bluebird china was simple, decaled rather than hand-painted, semi-porcelain dinnerware that was often inexpensive, and sometimes given away. To answer why Americans loved it and had to have it, consider the convergence of three factors: 1) America's enduring and virtually mystical romance with bluebirds; 2) the naively optimistic outlook prevailing in the 1920s in America; and 3) a giant leap in the influence of advertising brought about by the introduction of the radio along with marketing based upon the use of premiums and coupons.

Our country's love of bluebirds goes all the way back to native Americans who gave the bluebird a place of reverence in their folklore and society. Columbus and his men were delighted when they spotted their first bluebird, native only to North America and Bermuda. Early settlers found their appearance, playful personality, and beautiful song to be at once stimulating and pacifying. Little bluebirds were treated as part of the family and their long awaited arrival in the spring, a cause for celebration. The bluebird was seen not only as a symbol of happiness, beauty, and music, but of rebirth and renewal as well. While the eagle has long symbolized the strength and courage that is the backbone of the American spirit, the little bluebird came to represent our hope, spirit, and soul.

As America turned the corner from the nineteenth to the twentieth century, the bluebird began to be seen more and more in popular culture. A 1913 children's book by Georgette LeBlanc coined the term "The Bluebird of Happiness" and almost immediately the phrase became part of our vocabulary. Appearances in songs, magazines, art and yes, china, became tangible manifestations of the bluebird's place in America's heart. As we fought the "War to End All Wars" and moved into the unbridled optimism of the "Roaring '20s," it is no surprise that bluebird china enjoyed the zenith of its popularity. And as the Great Depression began to ensnare the American collective consciousness, while a dose of the bluebird spirit could certainly have helped, the time had come for the end of the bluebird china craze of that time. The wonderful message of hope, rebirth and life that bluebird china always

embodied then lay in hibernation to be discovered only recently by you, the modern carriers of the gentle bluebird message.

Definition of Bluebird China

Bluebird China is defined as any white porcelain or semi-porcelain decorated with one of many decals featuring bluebirds. The china first appeared in the late 1800s, was virtually everywhere in the early to mid-1920s, began phasing out in the late 1920s and was almost entirely gone by 1930. Shapes vary from manufacturer to manufacturer but the same decals appear without regard to manufacturer. For many years we pondered the question "Why do the same decals appear on the bluebird treatments of so many different manufacturers? What about patent infringement and copyright laws?" Finally, we realized that the Ohio Valley potteries were *buying* their decals, not *designing* them. The companies selling the decals included such companies as the Meyercord Decal Company located in Chicago. There is virtually no historical information available about the mysterious origin of the decal designs. Questions may always remain about the artists who drew the decals and the companies who sold them.

Bluebird China as Premiums

Green Stamps, Gold Stamps, coupons, box tops, "Free inside this box!" American merchandising has long embraced the premium as a marketing tool. Shortly after the Civil War, the nation's large retailers began to issue coupons that customers collected to redeem for items typically displayed in the store. These coupons were the predecessors of trading stamps that were to become ubiquitous in the U. S. after World War II.

The Grand Union Tea Company, The Great Atlantic and Pacific Tea Company and The Larkin Soap Company were among the first to emphasize the use of premiums. Premiums were initially available free with the purchase of products or based on accumulation of the required number of coupons, but later required a small cash outlay along with the coupons. The premiums could also usually be bought solely with cash and many of the premium programs developed lives of their own as free standing retailing enterprises. In the case of The Larkin Soap Company, the premium catalog outlived the soap merchandising by several decades.

The purveyors of premiums touted the idea that they purchased their basic inventory in such quantity (thereby getting a lower price) that they could sell the consumer the same item that the smaller retailer could at the same or lower price and give away the premium. They were typically quite proud of their achievement, attributing it to cutting out the profits of various "middlemen." Not so strongly stressed was the strategy that once a customer began saving coupons to trade for a coveted premium, they were more likely to be repeat buyers and develop a loyalty to the premium merchant. Much of the bluebird china in this book, although quite valuable today, began life literally as a give away item.

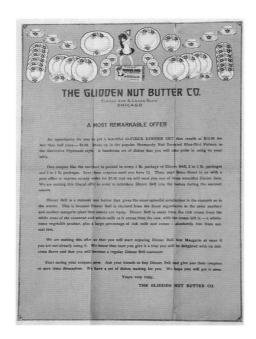

Purpose of this Book

This book is not intended to be a history of the various potters and their marks. Other books have done that quite well. This book discusses only the bluebird treat-ments done by the potters we have listed. We have attempted to address the availability and quality of each company's bluebird china but the book is not intended to be a complete encyclopedia of all the bluebird china manufactured or presently available. That would be impossible considering that there were at one time more than 300 potters in East Liverpool alone, all of which may have produced bluebird china at one time or another before they shut their doors forever.

Regarding the Stated Values

The market for bluebird china today is soaring like the little bluebirds depicted in the decals. There seems to be virtually no limit to how much collectors will pay for unusual pieces in good condition. Prices listed in this book are based on prices realized in Internet auctions, antique malls, flea markets and live auctions. We have attempted to eliminate the high and low end prices to arrive at a somewhat average price for the pieces described.

Condition

Bluebird china was not put away in the china cabinet for special occasions. It was used! So many of the pieces are crazed from setting in the oven too long or cracked, broken and faded from a few too many uses. This wear, however, does not render them valueless. There is a market for any piece of bluebird china, regardless of the condition. Even broken bluebird china is valuable, since it is often used in the making of jewelry or mosaics. In other words, never throw a piece away. It will always find a loving home.

Why We Collect Today

During the past ten years, in the process of doing research for this book and accumulating our own collection, we've asked collectors, "How did you get interested in bluebird china?" The answers always involve a loved one—grandmother, mother, aunt, sister, friend—who served them meals on "everyday" bluebird china. Some typical comments: From North Dakota, "My maternal grandmother had a few pieces I loved as I child. My mother, born in 1901, and her brother sold greeting cards door to door in order to get a few pieces from the greeting card company for their mother." From Louisiana, "I was born in 1912 and my mother died when I was four. I went to live with my grandmother in Virginia who had bluebird dishes as her every day dishes. When I see bluebirds on anything, my heart skips a beat." Ultimately, although there are as many reasons for collecting as there are collectors, through our love of bluebird china, we take ourselves back to a time of innocence, when our hopes and our bluebirds were both abundant.

Albright China Company

Albright China Company operated in Carrollton, Ohio, from about 1910 to 1930 with a second plant in Scio, Ohio, during the 1920s. Albright produced several varieties of bluebird china during the late 1900s to mid 1920s using two or three different decals and several different shapes and levels of embossing. Plates, cups and saucers, dinner plates, covered casseroles, creamers and sugars are all available as well as several sizes of platters. Some of Albright's pieces were stenciled with names of businesses, most likely given away in promotions. Most Albright China is medium to good quality.

Albright mark #1, early, probably up to 1925.

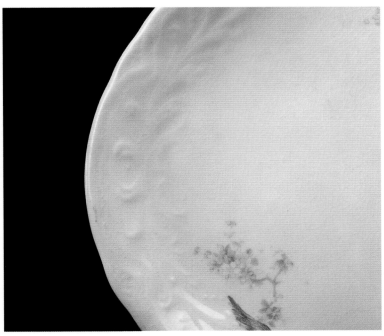

Albright mark #2, from the 1920s.

This is obviously one of Albright's earliest bluebird platters with fancy embossing and an ornate shape. Note also that the flowers on this decal are much smaller than those that followed. Mark #2. $115.

Platter, 13" x 10", with haphazardly drawn inner rim and imperfect shape, c. 1924. Mark #2. $75.

A very simple small ironstone platter, 10-1/2" x 8". Mark #1. $75.

Regular cup and saucer. Mark #2. $40.

Very plain, unrimmed dinner plates, c. 1925. Mark #1. $30 each.

Unusual cup and saucer from child's set. Mark #2. $65.

Large sugar bowl, heavily rimmed in gold, in excellent condition, c. 1924. Mark #2. $60.

High quality white ironstone bowl with bluebird treatment, dated 1924. Mark #2. $85.

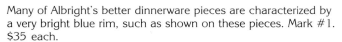

Many of Albright's better dinnerware pieces are characterized by a very bright blue rim, such as shown on these pieces. Mark #1. $35 each.

Singing bluebird decal, early 1920s.

Bottom of butter dish with unusual and not particularly popular decal of bluebirds in basket, c. 1925. Mark #2. $30.

Close-up of decal appearing on butter dish bottom above.

Anchor Pottery Company

Anchor Pottery Company was formed in 1893 in one of the major pottery centers in the country, Trenton, New Jersey. In 1900 the pottery boasted it was "one of the largest and best planned and equipped plants in the country" (The Board of Trade, *Industrial Trenton and Vicinity*, 1900). Anchor operated until 1926 when it was bought by Fulper Pottery Company. Anchor's bluebird china was produced as a premium for the Grand Union Tea Company, headquartered in New York City, with chain stores throughout the country. Anchor's bluebird china appeared early, probably around 1910. It is a fabulous heavy ironstone-type semi-porcelain and it is very hard to find.

Anchor Pottery mark, 1904-1912.

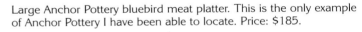

Large Anchor Pottery bluebird meat platter. This is the only example of Anchor Pottery I have been able to locate. Price: $185.

Atlas China Company and Atlas-Globe China Company

Atlas China Company of Niles, Ohio, produced an outstanding art deco looking bluebird china during the period 1922 to 1927. In 1927, Atlas China Company merged with Globe Pottery Company to form Atlas-Globe China Company. The new company continued to pro-duce bluebird dinnerware for a short time after the merger but it was much plainer than the Atlas China Company bluebird treatment. Unfortunately, very little Atlas bluebird or Atlas-Globe bluebird has survived and the pieces remaining are often unmarked.

Atlas China Company mark, 1922-27.

Atlas China Company's paneled shape, art-deco lines, beautiful gold rimming and vibrant colors are apparent in this grouping of dinnerware. Dinner plates, $45. Saucers, $20. Small bowl, $35.

Gold-rimmed, six-sided and paneled creamer and sugar, a rare find. $200 set.

Small plates with bright, royal blue rim, petite birds on the decals, $35 each.

Close-up of blue rim and delightful petite bluebirds on Atlas China bread and butter plates.

Twelve-sided Atlas China Dinner Plate with outer gold rim and inner blue rim. $40.

Close-up of Atlas China Company decal and edging. Time and use have faded the original gold outer-edge but the elegance of the original treatment is still apparent.

Atlas-Globe China Company Mark, 1927.

After Atlas China Company merged with Globe Pottery Company in 1927, the new company continued a bluebird dinnerware treatment for a brief period. This dinner plate is an example of the Atlas-Globe China Company bluebird china. $35.

Flowers and birds' breast are peach-colored rather than pink in the Atlas-Globe bluebird treatment. Edges of dinner plates were embossed but not colored with either gold or blue.

Edwin Bennett Pottery Company

Edwin Bennett established his pottery company in Baltimore, Maryland, in 1846 after working with his brother, James, in East Liverpool, Ohio. The Edwin Bennett Pottery Company operated for 90 years, but did not survive the depression. The company filed for bankruptcy in 1937. Bennett's double-glazed bluebird dinnerware appeared in the 1920's and, although uncommon today, it ranks among the most beautiful bluebird china ever produced.

Bennett's mark found on double-glazed dinnerware, manufactured in the 1920s.

Close-up of baby bluebird decal on covered casserole.

Generously applied decals characterize this superb dinnerware pattern, c. 1920. *Courtesy of Joan Sloat, Now and Then Shoppe, Fort Smith, Arkansas.* $275

A set of six-inch plates with more common decal. $30 each.

A heavy and enduring gold border encircles most of Bennett's beautiful dinnerware. 7.5" soup bowl, c. 1920. $45.

Design used exclusively by Edwin Bennett Pottery Company, c. 1890-1897. It appears on Bennett's early, coarse dinnerware and also on pitcher and bowl sets made before the turn of the century. Saucer, $15.

5.5" soup bowl, c. 1920. $35.

This mark was used by Edwin Bennett Pottery company c. 1890-1897. May have the words "ALBA CHINA" written underneath the globe. Pitcher and bowl set marked "ALBA," not pictured, $1250.

Buffalo Pottery

Buffalo Pottery was founded in 1902 by John Larkin, primarily to design and produce china and pottery for Larkin's hugely successful soap manufacturing enterprise. Buffalo Pottery (later Buffalo Company) produced a vast array of highly popular premiums for Larkin that helped to make Larkin Soap Manufacturing Company and its "Sweet Home Soap" a phenomenon.

Buffalo Erie County Historical Society.

Buffalo Erie County Historical Society.

Among the most popular of the premiums manufactured by Buffalo Pottery for Larkin were the bluebird pieces. Bluebird pitchers and a butter tub with drainer were first introduced as a premium in the 1918-1919 Larkin catalogs and a bluebird tea set consisting of tea plates, cups and saucers, sugar and creamer appeared in 1919-1922. Apparently a few other pieces, never pictured in the catalogs, could be special-ordered during that time including small bowls and a baby dish. Considering how brief the period of Buffalo bluebird production, it is amazing so much survives today. We suppose, because of its superior quality and beauty, Buffalo's bluebird was cherished and protected more than any other bluebird dinnerware.

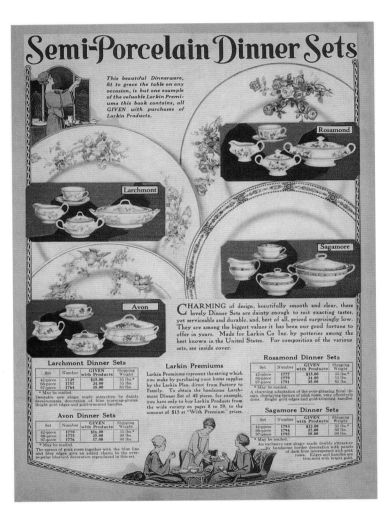

Buffalo Erie County Historical Society.

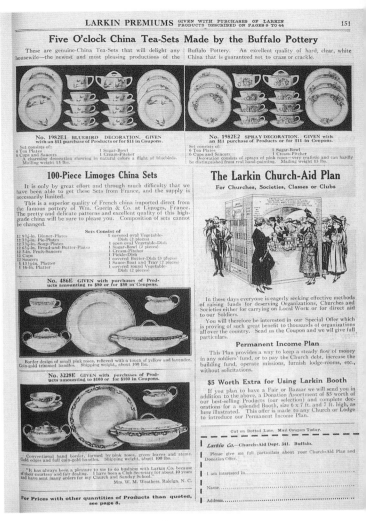

Buffalo Erie County Historical Society.

After 1922, Larkin premium catalogs continued to feature bluebird china, their "Avon" pattern, but instead of being manufactured by Buffalo China, this 97-piece set of dinnerware was described as coming "from one of the best known potteries in the United States" and "shipped from a factory in eastern Ohio." The undisclosed eastern Ohio pottery company was probably Homer Laughlin, based upon the shapes and decorations.

In addition to making Larkin bluebird premiums Buffalo China Company sold bluebird dinnerware to restaurants, institutions and many "Bluebird Cafés" throughout the country who special ordered their china with bluebird decals. Fortunately, all Buffalo bluebird pieces are dated and marked, making identification and research comparatively easy.

BLUE BIRD INN — BATAVIA, N.Y.

One of the many "Bluebird" establishments of the time.

Buffalo Pottery Company mark, c. 1918-1919. Appears on large and small pitchers.

Buffalo China Company mark, 1919.

"Splendid" is the description in the 1918 Larkin catalog and it is still a fitting description today. 6.75" water pitcher, $250. 4.5" cream pitcher, $200.

Butter tub and drainer, 5"diameter, c. 1918. $100.

Cup and saucer from Five O'clock Bluebird China Tea Set, 1919. $45.

Close-up of spectacular Buffalo bluebird.

Cup and saucer from Five O'clock Bluebird China Tea Set, 1920. $40. Note how the color has changed from the previous year.

Sugar bowl and cream pitcher from Buffalo's Five O'clock Bluebird China Tea Set. Sugar bowl with lid, $85. Cream pitcher, $65.

A comparison of the 1919 (right) and 1920 (left) cups and saucers clearly shows how the bluebirds became a lighter blue after 1919.

A small bowl, possibly part of the 1920 Five O'clock Tea Set. Is it just me or have the birds changed directions on the 1920 treatment? $40.

A tea plate and saucer from the 1919 Five O'clock Tea Set. Plate, $45. Saucer, $15.

This extremely rare baby plate by Buffalo never appeared in a premium catalog, c. 1920 but is reported to have been a Larkin giveaway. $150.

Large covered casserole, possibly restaurant china, could be the only one around today, dated 1920. $250.

Large meat platter, dated 1920. All birds are flying toward the center of the platter in this unusual decal placement. $125.

Two meat platters, c. 1920, possibly restaurant pieces. Large platter, $125. Medium platter, $85.

Three sizes of plates, dated 1920. Large dinner plate, $60. Medium plate, $50. Small plate, $40.

Rare and delightful single egg cup. Like the casserole pictured far left, this may be the only one. $75.

A match holder? The more familiar "chubby bluebird" decorates this mysterious restaurant piece. $150.

Unusual oval serving bowl, dated 1920. $75.

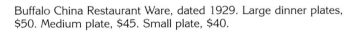

Buffalo China Restaurant Ware, dated 1929. Large dinner plates, $50. Medium plate, $45. Small plate, $40.

A different chubby bluebird treatment from a restaurant in New York, c. 1920. Small platter, $25.

Fancy Buffalo China nut or candy dishes, restaurant ware, c. 1920. $35 each.

Canisters (Cereal Jars and Spice Jars)

America was well into the depression when these mostly-unmarked, utilitarian pieces became popular. Gone is the lightheartedness of the chubby little baby bluebird decals typical of Homer Laughlin bluebird dinnerware and the optimism of the bluebirds soaring ever upward as portrayed in K T & K dinnerware. The bluebird decals appearing on these canister sets are somber birds in flight and determined bluebirds migrating in winter.

These jars (as they were originally named) are comparatively available although not often found in great condition. Expect chips, especially on lids.

This set of six square spice canisters was almost certainly made by A. E. Hull Pottery Company of Crooksville, Ohio. There is no mark. Set of six $125.

Again, the square shapes are indicative of spice canisters manufactured by A. E. Hull Pottery Company. This decal, a favorite on canister sets, appeared first in the 1920s but was never very popular on dinnerware. $35 each.

Large square coffee, tea, sugar and rice jars, probably produced by Hull Pottery Company. Matches the smaller spice jars pictured above. $50 each.

The large flour canister, probably Hull, with "migrating bluebirds in winter" decal.

Very crudely made round spice jars with ill-fitting lids, unmarked. $25 each.

Large round canisters, cleverly stacked, unmarked, poor quality. $40 each.

Better quality, matching large and small canisters with looped handles on lids and printing rather than cursive writing, unmarked. Note the molded bottoms to create "feet." Rice and tea jars, $75 each. Nutmeg jar, $40.

Yelloware spice set. Unmarked. Set of six, $150.

Another large canister treatment with looped handles and "feet." $75 each.

Matching oil and vinegar jars, unmarked, probably A. E. Hull Pottery Company. $50 each.

Oil and vinegar jars, probably made by A. E. Hull Pottery Company. $50 each.

Square salt box with wooden lid, unmarked. $150.

Mark on Czechoslovakian bluebird canisters.

Square salt box with wooden lid, double-decal application, un-marked. $150.

Czechoslovakian-made salt box with bluebird. $50.

Czechoslovakian bluebird pepper jar. $35.

Canonsburg Pottery

Canonsburg China Company, later Canonsburg Pottery, had a long history of continuing operations in Canonsburg, Pennsylvania, before it closed in 1978. The Company, founded in 1909 by John George, nephew of W. S. George, produced several varieties of high quality bluebird china during the 1920s, none with the ordinary bluebird treatments. Canonsburg's bluebird pieces are relatively available and inexpensive.

Canonsburg dinner plate, mark #1, c. 1918. $40. This same treatment also appears on an extremely hard-to-find grill plate, $175. The bluebird grill plate (not shown) is possibly the most valuable plate Canonsburg ever produced.

Close-up of decal on dinner plate above. Although similar to a decal used by K T & K, this particular placement is uniquely Canonsburg's.

Canonsburg's mark #1, 1909-1920s.

Canonsburg's mark #2, 1920s.

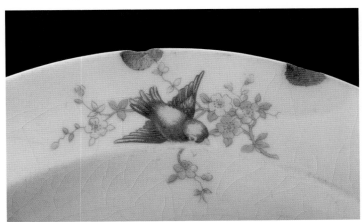

Three sizes of bowls, mark #1. Serving bowl, $30. Salad bowl, $25. Fruit bowl, $20.

High quality platter, c. 1920. Mark #1, $45.

This cup and saucer capture the beauty of this particular bluebird treatment. $40 set.

Close-up of unusual Canonsburg decal. Canonsburg was one of the very few potters to use this decal. I have seen it on only one other unmarked set which sadly lacked the Canonsburg quality.

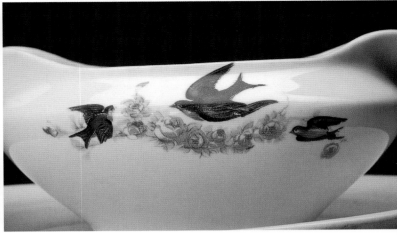

Canonsburg gravy with underplate, mark #1, c. 1920. $55.

Close-up of rather unattractive Canonsburg decal on gravy at left.

Close-up of decal with bluebirds among orange and blue flowers. This same decal appears most frequently on Homer Laughlin's Newell shape.

Dinner plate with scalloped rim, c. 1925. Mark #2, no trim on edges, $25.

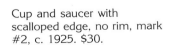
Cup and saucer with scalloped edge, no rim, mark #2, c. 1925. $30.

Carrollton Pottery Company

Carrollton Pottery Company of Carrollton, Ohio, is well-known for their unique dinnerware shapes. The company, established in 1903 and gone, like most others, before 1940, left behind a brilliant legacy of creative and innovative designs. Perhaps, a higher than average demand for Carrollton's bluebird when first introduced in the 1920s may help explain why there is a relatively large number and variety of pieces still available today. Collectors love Carrollton bluebird so expect to pay more.

Carrollton Pottery Company mark #1, 1920s.

Carrollton Pottery Company mark #2, with "H" in diamond, 1920s.

Carrollton's covered casserole, a real prize for any bluebird collector, c. 1925. *Courtesy of Stephanie and Tom Trambaugh.* $300.

Gravy and creamer, rimmed in blue, outstanding design, c. 1925. Gravy, $100. Creamer, $75. Sugar, not pictured, $95.

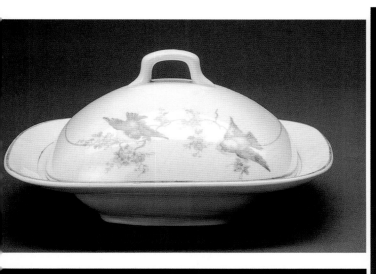

Carrollton's classic butter dish with cover, c. 1925. $250.

Dinner plate with inner and outer blue rim, c. 1925. $55. Matching cup and saucer, not pictured, $55.

Large bluebird treatment on dinner plate, c. 1920. $35.

Close up of the two bluebird decals used in Carrollton's dinnerware.

Two outstanding Carrollton platters, c. 1925. Large platter, $200. Medium platter, $150. Small platter, not pictured, $75.

Large pitchers are always difficult to locate. Finding one by Carrollton, almost unbelievable. Water pitcher, 6", c. 1925. $375.

Bowl, 7.5 inches, c. 1925. $50.

Serving bowl, c. 1925. $70.

Cartwright Bros. Pottery Company

Cartwright Bros. Pottery Company had a factory in East Liverpool, Ohio, from 1864 to 1924. Apparently, Cartwright Bros. produced an attractive and fancy line of bluebird dinnerware but the only evidence we have is a page from their catalog provided by the East Liverpool Museum of Ceramics.

Although I've searched far and wide, I have never found a Cartwright Bros. Pottery bluebird piece. Most may be unmarked. *Courtesy of Museum of Ceramics, East Liverpool, Ohio.*

Chippendale China

Chippendale China probably appeared a little before 1920, judging by the decal and shape. The two pieces I've seen are similar to early Saxon China but poorer quality and less attractive. "Chippendale China" may be the name of the company or it may be the name of the pattern. Like much in the history of bluebird china, Chippendale China remains something of a mystery.

Mysterious Chippendale China mark.

Dinner plate marked Chippendale China, $20.

Bluebird decal and placement are similar to Saxon China's.

Cleveland China Company and the George H. Bowman Company

"Cleveland China" was not a china manufacturer. Instead, it was the mark placed on dinnerware sold and distributed by the George H. Bowman Company of Cleveland, Ohio. Pieces marked "Cleveland China" could have been made by any number of different potters during the period 1890s to 1930s. Bluebird dinnerware bearing the "Cleveland China" mark is generic but lovely, very similar in quality and design to Homer Laughlin's bluebird treatment. Give credit to George Bowman for being quite a salesman – Cleveland China items show up everywhere and often. Most is moderately priced.

Cleveland China mark, c. 1920.

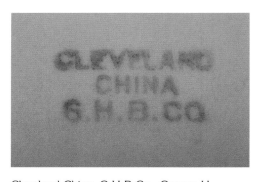

Cleveland China, G H B Co., George H. Bowman Company mark, c. 1925.

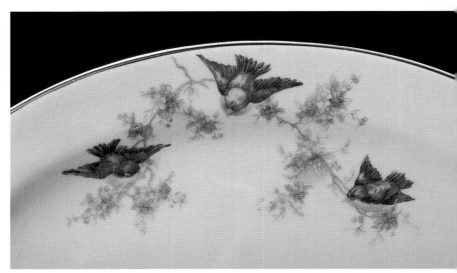

Cleveland's bluebird decal, characterized by very vibrant blue-winged birds and bright pink blossoms.

Two sizes of Cleveland China plates, rimmed in bright blue. 10" plate, $40. 6.5" plate, $25.

A grouping of Cleveland China platters of various sizes. 10.5" platter, $70. 12" platter, $75. 12.5" platter, $75.

The shape of this Cleveland China gravy is identical to Homer Laughlin's "Kwaker." Could this have been made by Homer Laughlin for George Bowman? Or, just a Homer Laughlin imitator? Gravy, $110.

Careful attention to decal placement, bright white china and dark vibrant blue rim characterize Cleveland's bluebird treatment. Small bowl, $40.

Pair of cups and saucers, marked Cleveland China, $40 each set.

According to the provenance on this rare child's plate and mug, it was a gift from "Daddy, to his little girl" in 1919, $300.

Simply elegant Cleveland China covered casserole, $250.

Clinchfield Pottery and Southern Potteries Inc.

Clinchfield Pottery began in Erwin, Tennessee, in 1917 and was incorporated in 1920 as Southern Potteries, Inc. One of the early lines of dinnerware produced at Clinchfield was their particular "southern" style of blue-bird china. Clinchfield's bluebird has a thick, heavy, al-most unrefined feel and is not nearly as well-done as some of its East Liverpool counterparts. However, what Clinchfield lacks in quality, it makes up for in design. It is large, curvy, highly embossed and very loveable as evidenced by the recent sky-high market for Clinchfield.

Very early Clinchfield Chinaware mark #1, in red, c. 1917-1918.

S. P. I. Clinchfield China mark #3, c. 1917-1920.

Clinchfield China mark #2, 1920s.

Very early, c. 1918. Clinchfield creamer, mark #1. $125.

Fancy platter, bluebirds in a garland of roses decal, c. 1920. Mark #3. $95.

Fancy Clinchfield dinner plate, dated 1925. $50.

Close-up of bluebirds in a garland of roses decal.

Another early, c. 1917, bluebird treatment. Mark #3. Small plates, $40 each.

Close-up of decal on platter at left.

This is a later bluebird platter, c. 1927. Owen-Minerva China Company popularized this decal. Large platter in poor condition, $35.

Breathtaking large covered casserole, c. 1920. $275.

Close up of decal and embossing on covered casserole.

Covered butter with cover, dated 1925, $150.

Colonial Pottery Company

Colonial Pottery Company operated in East Liverpool from 1903 to 1929. For a company with so little written history, Colonial's early dinnerware shapes are surprisingly elegant and sophisticated. Colonial bluebird usually sells for below-average prices when available, which isn't often.

Colonial Sterling China mark, 1910 to 1919. This mark also appears on flow blue dinnerware and game sets as well as some commemorative plates manufactured by Colonial Pottery Company.

Colonial Pottery Company mark, eagle and bell, 1915-1929.

Butter with cover, Colonial Sterling mark, dated 1915, $150.

Another Colonial Sterling butter with cover, this one dated 1919, $150.

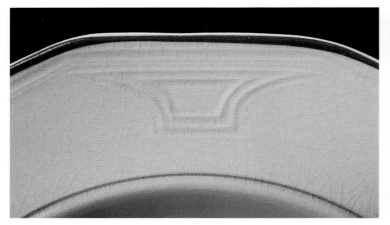

Creamer with outstanding shape and design, c. 1915. $50.

Close up of decal and embossing on art-deco butter dish pictured on page 45.

The only bluebird coffeepot I have ever seen! Gorgeous ironstone shape, marked Colonial Sterling China, 1918. $200.

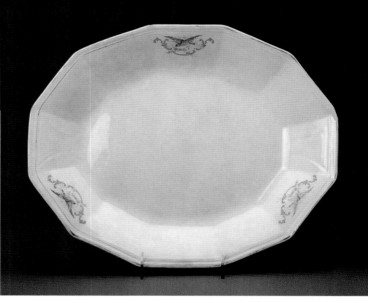

Colonial Sterling twelve-sided, gold rimmed dinnerware. All part of a service for twelve dated 1918. Platter, $50. 10" dinner plate, $25. 6" plate, $15. 7.5" bowl, $25. 5.5" bowl, $15.

Colonial Sterling, twelve-sided, paneled cup and saucer, dated 1918. $35.

Close up of bluebird in cartouche decal used on Colonial Sterling dinnerware. Most of the gold rim has worn away. This decal was also used extensively by Salem China Company in the mid-to-late 1920s.

A butter pat came with every serving. Unmarked but definitely part of this same set. $20 each.

Medium ironstone platter, eagle with bell mark, c. 1920. $45.

Colonial ironstone dinner plate with molded inner and rim eagle with bell mark, c. 1920. Beautiful quality, $40.

Crescent China Company

Crescent China Company of Alliance, Ohio, c. 1920-1927, was predecessor to Leigh Potters, Inc. and owned by the Sebring brothers who were involved with numerous other pottery companies of the time. Crescent's bluebird is magnificent but uncommon. In ten-plus years of collecting, we've seen only two pieces with the Crescent mark.

Crescent China Company mark, c. 1920-1925.

Six-sided covered vegetable, unique Crescent design, unsurpassed quality, c. 1925. $250.

Crooksville China Company

Crooksville China Company operated in Crooksville, Ohio, from 1902 to 1959. The bluebird china produced at their factory in the mid 1920s ranks among the best, characterized by clever shapes, appealing decal applications and an extra high grade of china. For sweetness and charm, I would choose Crooksville's bluebird over all others. Apparently, so would many other collectors. Crooksville's bluebird is scarce and ultra-expensive.

This 10" x 13" Crooksville platter, decorated with nine bluebirds, is the quintessential piece of bluebird china , c. 1925. $350.

Crooksville China mark, c. 1920s-1930s. This is the only mark I have seen on Crooksville China bluebird.

Bowl, 7.5", with beautiful royal blue border, c. 1925. *Courtesy of Joan Sloat, Now and Then Shoppe, Ft. Smith, Arkansas.* $75.

Rare 6" plate, rimmed in gold, souvenir of "Zanesville District Conference. Crooksville M. E. Church, November 22-23, 1931, Franklin McElfares D. D., District Superintendent." $100.

Crown Potteries Company

Crown Potteries Company, Evansville, Indiana, began production in 1891 and did not close its doors until 1954. The Company introduced a basic line of bluebird china sometime in the early 1920s and kept it in production for many years without changing it. Not until the 1940s do you find another Crown Potteries bluebird treatment.

Demand for Crown bluebird must have been strong and stable like the dinnerware itself. There are still enough plates, platters, bowls, cups, and saucers around to put together an entire dinner set and most is in exceptionally good condition. Prices are moderate, comparable to Homer Laughlin

Crown Potteries Mark from 1920s to 1930s. The date will sometimes appear below the crown.

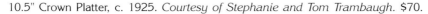

10.5" Crown Platter, c. 1925. *Courtesy of Stephanie and Tom Trambaugh.* $70.

Three flat soup bowls, $55 each. Two large serving bowls, 9.25" x 3", $70 each. *Courtesy of Stephanie and Tom Trambaugh.*

Coveted children's set consisting of four cups/saucers, four plates, round serving platter, oval platter, round bowl, oval bowl, creamer and sugar and the prized child-sized covered casserole. $900 set.

Comparison of sugar bowl and cream pitcher in child's set with regular sugar and cream pitcher. The children's pieces were never done to scale. Child's creamer, $75. Adult creamer, $50. Child's sugar bowl, $85. Adult sugar bowl, $55.

Crown Pottery's child-sized vegetable casserole in un-played with condition. A million thanks to the little girl who owned this one! *Courtesy of Stephanie and Tom Trambaugh.* $250.

Grouping of Crown Pottery dinnerware from 1920s. Medium platter, $60. Dinner plate, $40. Serving bowl, $50. Small bowls, $25 each. Creamer, $50. Sugar bowl, $55.

A Crown Pottery bluebird punch bowl, 9.5" x 5.75"! This may be the largest piece of bluebird china ever made and the only one in existence today. *Courtesy of Stephanie and Tom Trambaugh.* $550.

Exceptional milk pitcher, 6" x 9.5", $400.

Two Crown Pottery advertising plates, dated 1926. One reads "Compliments of A. F. Ziegenhorn, Claytonville, Ill." and the other "Wm. I. Keithahn, Walnut, Ill." $50 each.

This bluebird design, known as their "Good Luck" pattern was originated by Crown in the 1940s. Dinner plates, $20 each.

ELPCO

The East Liverpool Potteries Company, ELPCO, was an association of several East Liverpool Potters who combined their efforts in order to better compete with the larger companies and imported wares. It was in existence until 1907 or so according to a list compiled by the Carnegie Library of East Liverpool, Ohio. The ELPCO mark, however, continued to be used by the United States Pottery Company of Wellsville, Ohio, which was one of the members of the East Liverpool Potteries Company. All of the bluebird pieces pictured here are dated in the 1920s and so were probably the product of the United States Pottery Company. Every piece of ELPCO bluebird I've found has been dated from 1920 to 1926. ELPCO's china is very white, high quality and desirable. Their baby plates are a real treat for collectors.

The ELPCO china mark used by the United States Pottery Company of Wellsville, Ohio, in the 1920s.

Bottom of ELPCO butter dish, dated 1920. $40.

10" x 13" ELPCO platter, dated 1921. $125.

Beautifully styled ELPCO gravy boat, dated 1921. $85.

ELPCO sugar bowl and creamer, looped handles,
dated 1921. Set, $160.

Covered vegetable casserole, dated 1921. $175.

Small berry bowl, dated 1921. $40.

Two "D is for Dog" baby plates, slightly different sizes and
decal applications, one is from 1925 and the other from
1926. $175 each.

Baby plate with turkey, dated 1925.
*Compliments of Joan Sloat, Now
& Then Shoppe, Ft. Smith,
Arkansas.* $150.

Baby plate with kittens, dated 1925. $175.

Baby plate with pigs, dated 1926. *Courtesy of Patti Mainard-Miller.* $150.

Baby plate with bunnies in absolutely perfect condition, dated 1923. $175.

ELPCO baby plate with faded blue birds, c. 1925. $75.

Not pictured. The elephant baby plate, c. 1925. $150.

European Efforts

The burgeoning American pottery industry of the early twentieth century certainly traced its roots directly to the long standing tradition of European ceramic manufacture and artistry. While the bluebird china craze had its roots in America, the European china companies quickly recognized the growing appeal of the product and jumped on the bandwagon. Although there were clearly similarities between American bluebird china and its European counterparts, the European treatments definitely had their own style. The birds were slightly different in their physical appearance and the Europeans tended to introduce a few more colors into the pattern. Although there were many manufacturers of European bluebird china, the information regarding the details of the companies and their marks is much sketchier than it is with the American companies.

Victoria Austria Blue Bird mark. Most likely manufactured by Victoria Porcelain Factory, Altrohlav, Bohemia, c. 1891-1918.

Victoria Austria Teapot. Large single bluebird decal, c. 1918. $100.

Close-up of Victoria Austria decal. Victoria Austria was not shy about using this decal. It could be found on almost anything ceramic, from dinner ware to toiletry sets to decorative collectibles.

Victoria Austria candle holder. $25.

Victoria Austria scallop edge cup and saucer. $25.

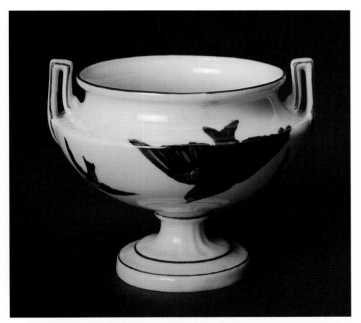

"O. M. Read Company – Fair Week 1914" advertising inscription on back of Victoria Austria Plate.

Victoria Austria pedestal sugar. $25.

Pair of small Victoria Austria plates. $20. each.

Boronian trio (cup, saucer and biscuit plate), interesting octagonal shape. $75.

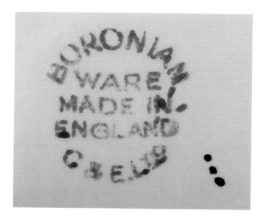

Boronian Ware mark. English.

Royal Stafford mark. Probably the work of Thomas Poole Co., Staffordshire, England. c. 1915-

Close-up of Boronian Ware decal.

Royal Stafford trio. Unusual flower placement on plate. $75.

Shelley mark. Shelley Potteries, Ltd., Staffordshire, England, 1925.

Close-up of Royal Stafford decal.

Close-up of Shelley decal.

Shelley creamer and open sugar, very art deco, highest quality china. $200.

Crown China mark. English.

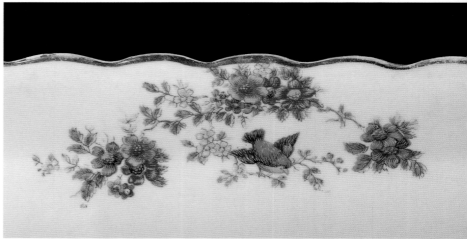

Close-up of Crown China decal. Cute bird with pale orange breast and vibrant orange and red flowers.

Crown China tray, cup and saucer. Fancy shape and gold edge. Tray $40. Cup and saucer $40.

BCM Clarence Ware grouping of four trios. $55 each trio.

BCM Clarence Ware mark. Made by the Co-Operative Wholesale Society, Ltd., Staffordshire, England.

Aynsley mark. John Aynsley and Sons, Staffordshire, England.

Close-up of BCM Clarence Ware decal. Heavy dose of flowers and very vibrant colors.

Close-up of Aynsley decal. Different sort of bird in flight, no flowers and tree branch apparently decorated with beads.

Roslyn Co. mark. England.

Roslyn Co. cake plate. Fancy shape, handled, interior placement of birds. $75.

Aynsley trio. $100.

Scotch Ivory mark. B. P. Co., Ltd. Great Britain.

Close-up of Scotch Ivory decal. Birds almost entirely blue with orange neck. Large pink roses and small blue flowers.

Scotch Ivory breakfast/tea set. Beautiful teapot. Bowl decal placement has birds almost kissing. Note the inclusion of the jelly with underplate. Very British. $475.

Four Scotch Ivory trios, with tulip border. $50 per trio.

Palissy mark. Albert & Jones, Ltd., Staffordshire, England, 1922.

Booth's mark. Booth's Silicon China, Staffordshire, England.

Palissy tea set. Low quality. $75.

Booth's octagonal plate. Large, menacing birds with green feathers. $25.

Four Royal Albert fancy edge plates. $30 each.

Rudolstadt mark. Most likely the work of the New York and Rudolstadt Pottery Co., Rudolstadt, Thuringia, Germany.

Royal Albert Crown China mark. Thomas C. Wild Co., Staffordshire, England.

Royal Albert open sugar. $50.

Rudolstadt uncovered sugar. $25.

French China Company

French China Company of Sebring, Ohio, (c. 1898-1929) was one of the most dominant, influential, innovative and definitely prolific of all the Ohio Valley pottery companies. French's first bluebird china treatment evolved from their highly popular flow blue dinnerware of the early twentieth century. The first bluebird treatment combined a decal of a large bluebird in flight with plates and platters edged in flow blue. As early as 1910, they dropped the flow blue altogether and began to manufacture bluebird decorated china in earnest. French bluebird was marketed effectively throughout the country and survives in mass quantities today. Some of the early pieces marked "La Francaise" are stunning and deserve the highest praise but most of the later pieces are of medium quality, at best. Prices for pieces marked "La Francaise" are about twice those for pieces marked "F. C. Company."

The fleur-de-lis mark of French China Company, c. 1905-1915.

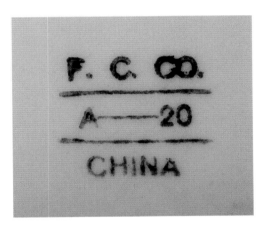

F. C. Co., another French China Company mark, almost always dated. "Martha Washington" indicates a shape of dinnerware, introduced c. 1917. Some Sebring China Company pieces are also marked "Martha Washington."

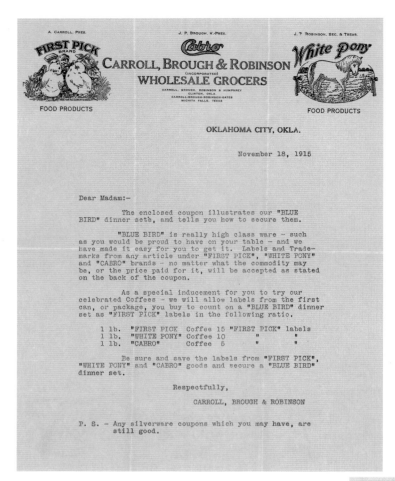

Labels and trademarks from any "First Pick," "Cabro," or "White Pony" brand could be exchanged for "the 42-piece Haviland Shape Blue Bird Pattern Dinner Sets." The coupon goes on to say "Blue Bird is a recognized new creation in China Decoration, and will appeal to your fancy. Large China and Department Store prices on these sets range in value for $6 to $9 each." With 50 labels, you could buy a set for $3.75, including shipping.

THIS IS WORTH READING

100% value in our food products, and a handsome set of China Ware, at our wholesale factory cost, plus car-load freight and cost of handling, given you, as follows:

Save the labels and trade-marks from any "FIRST PICK" goods, and when you have secured fifty (50), send or bring them, with $3.75 cash, and we will ship you one of the 42-piece Haviland Shape Blue Bird Pattern Dinner Sets, illustrated on other side.

Unlike cheap ware, "BLUE BIRD" is made from the choicest imported clay, and the decoration placed under the glazing—so it will not wear off—a point worth considering.

"BLUE BIRD" is a recognized new creation in China Decoration, and will appeal to your fancy. Large China and Department Store prices on these sets range in value from $6.00 to $9.00 each.

Our price to you, with fifty (50) "FIRST PICK" trade-marks, only $3.75.

We have substituted in this make-up larger pieces for the little Butter Chips—usually included.

"WHITE PONY" labels or trade-marks will be accepted in the ratio of 2 for 1 "FIRST PICK," and "CABRO" 3 for 1. This places our entire line of labels at your disposal and renders results quick and easy for all. No sets sold without labels.

Silverware coupons may be used, as usual, or may apply for China with equal value of "FIRST PICK" labels. Sets weigh about 35 lbs. each, and are sold F. O. B. our house. All breakage in transit replaced if reported promptly.

Send Labels, Drafts or Money Orders to the nearest address below.

CARROLL, BROUGH & ROBINSON, Oklahoma City, Okla.

CARROLL, BROUGH, ROBINSON & HUMPHREY, Clinton, Okla.

CARROLL, BROUGH, ROBINSON & GATES, Wichita Falls, Texas

The cup and saucer for sale with the coupon shown at left, c. 1915. $50.

This is one of French China Company's stunning pieces, medium platter with three rings of blue and two big birds in flight, c. 1915. $185.

Close-up of La Francaise bluebird decals.

Excellent large sugar bowl with looped handles, c. 1915. $85.

A grouping of four small La Francaise plates, illustrating very well how irresistible this pattern can be, $30 each.

Oval casserole, $200.

Double egg cups, unmarked, but most likely La Francaise. $60 each.

Round covered dish with lid, fancy and embossed, an early La Francaise piece, c. 1905. $200.

Large La Francaise sugar bowl, in "Priscilla" shape. $85.

A classic, La Francaise gravy, c. 1915. $110.

Large La Francaise platter, $175.

Covered casserole, "Martha Washington" shape, F. C. Company, $100.

Another bluebird treatment on "Martha Washington" shape. $100.

This unusual French Company bowl has embossed beading around the edges and molded tab handles. $45.

F. C. Company creamer and sugar with rare decal, bluebirds flying in blue flowers, c. 1925. Set, $125.

An earlier F. C. Company creamer and sugar with rare bluebirds in blue flowers decal, c. 1920. *Courtesy of Joan Sloat, Now & Then Shoppe, Ft. Smith, Arkansas.* In poor condition and missing lid, $30.

French China Company "Martha Washington" monogrammed "F" creamer and sugar, $35 set.

Angular "Martha Washington" sugar bowl with pudgy little bluebirds, $45.

Twelve-sided "Martha Washington" platter. French China Co. made "Martha Washington" dinnerware up until its dissolution in 1929. $45.

A very poor quality "Martha Washington" gravy. $20.

A beautiful covered casserole, F. C. Company mark, dated 1920. $150.

Unfortunately, another example of a low-quality "Martha Washington" piece. $15.

Creamer and sugar with looped handles and gold edges, F. C. Company mark, c. 1920. $80 set. This shape might also be marked "La Francaise."

W. S. George Pottery Company

W. S. George purchased the East Palestine Pottery Company in 1904 and thus began the W. S. George Pottery Company that rapidly expanded to include four plants by the late 1920s – two in East Palestine, Ohio, one in Canonsburg, Pennsylvania, and one in Kittanning, Pennsylvania. W. S. George Company continued into the 1950s, long after its colorful founder died in 1925. Bluebird decorations appear on the George's White Granite shape, c. 1915, Derwood shape, c. 1920, Radisson shape, c. 1920, and Lido shape, c. 1930. Most is of exceptional quality and priced accordingly.

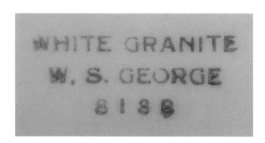

W. S. George Company, "White Granite" mark, c. 1915-1920.

W. S. George "White Granite" deep bowls, c. 1915. $75 each.

W. S. George "Derwood" mark, c. 1920.

5.5" "White Granite" pitcher, $125.

This bluebird decal was used exclusively by W. S. George and only on "Derwood" pieces.

Rare soap dish, probably from an early pitcher and bowl set, "White Granite" mark, c. 1915. $125.

Two pieces from the "Derwood" dinnerware set, featuring the unique W. S. George decal. Bowl, $40. Small plate, $35.

Large and small "Derwood" jugs, c. 1920 with two different bluebird treatments. Rare large jug, $150. Small jug, $60.

George "Derwood" cake plates, one with a very different bluebird decal. $125 each.

W. S. George "Derwood" oval and round covered casseroles. Both are in like-new condition after 80-plus years, a tribute to the workmanship of the W.S. George Company. Oval casserole with lid, $250. Round casserole with lid, $275.

Delightful, large "Derwood" sugar bowl with looped handles, c. 1915. $100.

George "Derwood" creamer and sugar, set $200.

The hard-to-find "Derwood" cup and saucer, $60.

"Derwood" dinner plate, $40. Soup bowls, $45 each.

W. S. George "Radisson" mark, c. 1910-1915.

"Radisson" plate, $50. "Radisson" was W. S. George's answer to Haviland's "Ransom" pattern.

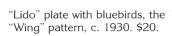

"Lido" plate with bluebirds, the "Wing" pattern, c. 1930. $20.

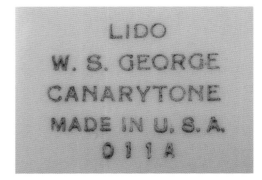

W. S. George "Lido" mark, c. 1930.

Greenwood China Company

Greenwood China Company of Trenton, New Jersey, c. 1868-1930, may have been the very first potter ever to use the bluebird decal. The ironstone platter below bears the incised Greenwood China mark that both Debolt and Lehner state was used around 1886 only. If so, this would be one of the earliest pieces of bluebird china manufactured anywhere. Greenwood China Company is best known for their simple, heavy and durable ironstone ware, marketed chiefly to hotels and restaurants at the end of the nineteenth century. This small, plain ironstone platter could definitely have been part of that early product line.

Impressed, rather than stamped, mark, c. 1886, according to Debolt.

Close-up of decal on the earliest known piece of bluebird china. Flowers have more cranberry than pink and birds are a darker blue, otherwise the same familiar and charming decal.

Platter, 11.5", c. 1886. Too rare to determine value.

Harker Pottery

Harker Pottery was among the earliest successful American pottery makers. It was founded by Benjamin Harker, who moved his family from England in the 1830s, purchasing a farm on the Ohio River at East Liverpool. Discovering abundant clay deposits on his farm, Harker initially sold clay to James Bennett (of Bennett Pottery Company) but soon determined that he could make pottery himself. Along with his sons, George and Benjamin, Jr., Harker began his company in East Liverpool in 1840. In 1931, the company moved to Chester, West Virginia, where it operated until 1972.

Harker Pottery was one of the first to use the bluebird decal, probably prior to 1900 and maybe as early as 1890. Harker also produced what are probably the record holders for the "most heavily bluebirded" pieces of china. Early Harker bluebird plates are decorated with twelve bluebirds – at least four more than any that followed! Acquiring a piece of Harker bluebird requires extreme diligence and patience for not only are you competing with bluebird china collectors but you will have just as many Harker Pottery collectors searching for the same piece. Finding the Harker arrow on a piece of bluebird china can be thrilling but expect to pay for it.

Harker Pottery Company Mark. c. 1890-1920.

Harker "Hotoven" mark, artistic in its own right. c. 1935.

Harker 12-bird dinner plate. You will not find more birds on one plate. Repaired, $50. If you can find a perfect one, $250.

Close-up of the early, c. 1890. Harker bluebird decal.

Harker large water pitcher, typical of the tasteful Harker shapes, c. 1890-1910. $350.

Perfect Harker creamer, c. 1900. *Courtesy of Stephanie and Tom Trambaugh.* $150.

Harker covered sugar, with stylish looped handles and lid, c. 1900. *Courtesy of Stephanie and Tom Trambaugh.* $175.

Large faceted serving bowl, c. 1900, scarce. $175.

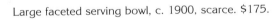

Medium salad/cereal bowl, with blue rim. $50.

Harker medium platter, fair condition, $60. In good condition, $150.

Harker cup and saucer, with extra bird and very nice dusty pink flowers. $50.

Harker "Hotoven" pieces, c. 1935. Completely different bird and foliage treatments. Bowl, $35. Covered casserole, $80.

Hopewell China Company

Hopewell China Company, also known as Ostrow China Company, was established by Sol Ostrow in Hopewell, Virginia, in 1920 or so. Hopewell was only a minor player in the pottery arena and could not withstand the depression. It was gone before 1930. Some of

Hopewell's bluebird china is quite desirable, characterized by pinker than usual tones in the typical bluebird decal. Most, however, is poor quality, especially the pieces marked "Ostrow." Their early platters and plates are worth acquiring, otherwise, there's probably not much of value.

Hopewell in circle, mark #1, c. 1925.

A third Hopewell mark, c. 1920-1925.

A second and the most common Hopewell mark, c. 1920-1929.

Hopewell mark #4, the Princess Anne Ostrow China mark, c. 1920-1929.

Medium platter, edged with dark blue rim, common Hopewell ship mark. $65.

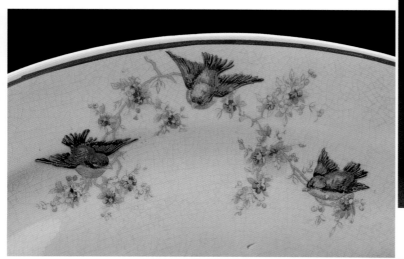

Close-up of Hopewell decal with pinker hues.

A pretty Hopewell plate, mark #3, dated 1921. $45.

Creamer, marked with Hopewell ship, c. 1925. $45.

Gravy with attached underplate, c. 1925. $100.

Plate, marked with Princess Anne Ostrow, c. 1929. $15.

Hopewell soup bowl, c. 1925. $30.

Illinois China Company

Illinois China Company produced bluebird china that was simple, elegant and high quality. In an industry over-populated with shooting stars, Illinois had staying power, operating for over twenty years. Nevertheless, their history remains somewhat cloudy. First located in either Whitehall or nearby Roodhouse, Illinois, the Company moved to its home in Lincoln, Illinois in 1919. The company was absorbed by the Stetson China Company in the 1940s. Illinois bluebird china is very uncommon and expensive.

Mark of the Illinois China Company, c. 1919-1946. During its existence, this is the only mark the Company ever used.

Pair of very nice dinner plates, c. 1920, with fancy embossed edge and six bluebird decals. Another American attempt to replicate the Haviland "Ransom" pattern. Dinner plates, $55 each.

Close-up of Illinois China Company's version of the standard bluebird decal showing the beautifully vibrant color, especially the flowers.

Embellished gravy bowl with typical Illinois attention to detail, c. 1920. $125.

Unusual little pickle dish with embossing, c. 1920. $85.

A magnificent though very worn Illinois platter, once again an imitation of Haviland's "Ransom" pattern. In poor condition, $45.

Covered sugar with looped handles, c. 1920. Lid has been repaired. In repaired condition, $50.

Imperial China

"Imperial China" was a name used by the Ohio China Company of East Palestine, Ohio, c. 1902-1912, and Pioneer Pottery Company of Wellsville, Ohio, c. 1885-1902. However, according to *Debolt's Dictionary of American Pottery Marks*, this particular "Imperial China" mark was probably not associated with either of the aforementioned companies. Debolt thought it could have been an early mark, c. 1910-1920, of the Limoges China Company of Sebring, Ohio. This one piece of bluebird marked "Imperial China" is reminiscent of French Company's early bluebird treatments. The maker, for now, remains uncertain.

The stamped Imperial China mark, c. 1910.

A tall, 7.5" water pitcher, crazed and cracked, c. 1910. *Courtesy of Joan Sloat, Now & Then Shoppe, Ft. Smith, Arkansas.* In poor condition, $45. In good condition, if you could find it, $200.

International Pottery Company

International Pottery Company of Trenton, New Jersey, was formed in 1860, and was originally the Lincoln Pottery. Under the British inspired name, Royal China, they produced a rather ordinary bluebird china, some of which was destined for hotel and restaurant use. Not much International bluebird is on the market today.

Royal China International mark, in circle, c. 1910.

Large, bluebird decal used by International. Varied considerably from batch to batch.

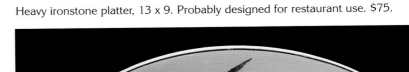

Heavy ironstone platter, 13 x 9. Probably designed for restaurant use. $75.

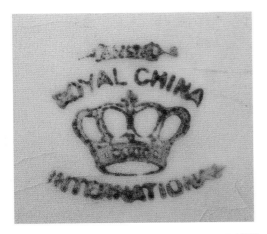

Royal China International, no circle, c. 1915-1930.

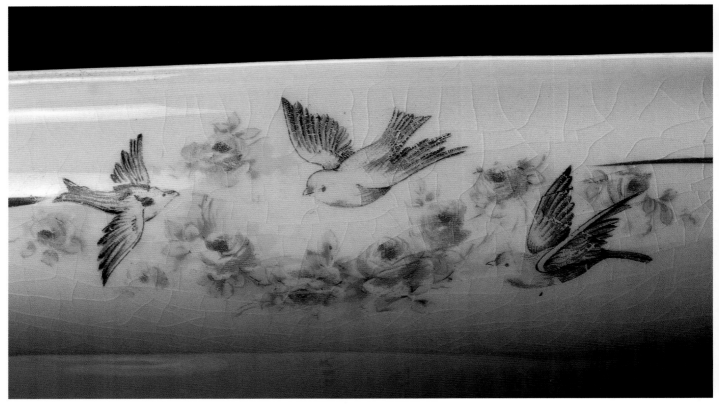

International oval covered casserole with extremely ill fitting lid. The flaws in these products could be the result of the company's rush to get them to market. $65.

Edwin M. Knowles China Company

Edwin M. Knowles China Company began production in 1901 across the river from East Liverpool, Ohio, in Chester, West Virginia. In their early ads, however, they claimed to be in East Liverpool, Ohio. Boldly, the company moved a little further south to Newell, West Virginia, and built a new facility in 1913. From then on the company thrived and attained huge success as a manufacturer of stylish vitrified dinnerware. It finally closed its doors in 1963. Bluebird china produced by Edwin M. Knowles in the 1920s is hard to find with the exception of the large meat platter. We've seen five or six of those in the last two years. Edwin M. Knowles has a huge following of collectors in competition with bluebird collectors for the unusual bluebird-decorated pieces. High demand and low supply always translate to high prices.

The Edwin M. Knowles mark on bluebird china, c. 1920.

Two small plates, marked Edwin M. Knowles, c. 1920. 5.5" plate, $35. 7.5" plate, $50.

Edwin Knowles meat platter "Mayflower" shape, 15" x 11.5", c. 1920. $200. Close up of decal on platter.

Attractive Knowles 13" x 10" platter with bright blue rim, $75.

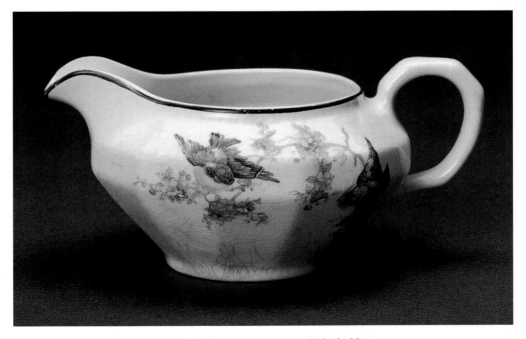

Edwin Knowles creamer, popular "Mayflower" shape, c. 1920. $100.

Knowles, Taylor & Knowles

Not long after its beginning in 1872, Knowles, Taylor & Knowles had established itself as the most prominent and successful china company in all of East Liverpool. Under the brilliant leadership of Isaac Knowles, the company grew and prospered becoming the largest pottery in America by 1881. According to Mary Frank Gaston's *Collector's Encyclopedia of Knowles, Taylor & Knowles China*, Isaac Knowles invented the first piece of machinery to be used in the pottery industry, a shaft driven jigger. Inventions, processes and techniques introduced at K T & K factories revolutionized the making of china and pottery in America. Sadly, K T & K, the pottery giant, unable to compete with Japanese imports, filed for bankruptcy in 1931.

K T & K decorated several dinnerware lines with bluebirds. Their most popular bluebird patterns are found on the "Victory," "Niana," and "America" shapes but are likely to show up on just about any piece marked "K T & K." Bluebird dinnerware sets are referred to as "Flying Blue Bird Dinner Sets" (1918), the "Blue Bird of Happiness Dinnerware" (1922), "Bluebird and Apple Blossom Set" (1923-24) and just "Bluebird Dinner Set" (1928). A wide and unusual array of pieces could be purchased for these sets including cheese and cracker dishes, chocolate pots and cups, handled and un-handled custards, muffin covers, muffin plates, ramekins, grapefruit bowls, jugs of many sizes, coffee pots with and without side handles, oyster tureens and the list goes on. K T & K bluebird china can be a lifetime study since there are so many new pieces constantly surfacing and most at affordable prices.

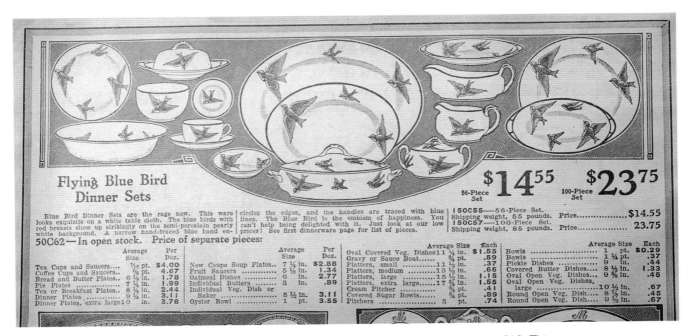

"Flying Blue Bird Dinner Sets" on K T & K's "Niana" dinnerware shape. Montgomery Catalog, 1918. This particular bluebird treatment was relatively expensive. The prices dropped in later years. The most expensive were the oval covered vegetable dish at $1.55 and the extra large 17.75" platter at $1.55. A tremendous amount of this particular line survives today although much is seriously crazed and brown.

"Blue Bird of Happiness" Dinnerware on K T & K's "Victory" dinnerware shape, Montgomery Catalog, 1922. This decal was used exclusively by K T & K. Covered butter dishes were the most expensive, $1.15 compared with a large platter which was $1.10. The large pitcher in this pattern is difficult to find today but you could have purchased in 1928 for 78 cents.

The "Victory" shape was back in 1928 on the "Bluebird Dinner Set." Prices had increased, however. The same 12 cups and saucers that cost $4.25 in 1922 cost $4.50 in 1928. The "Victory" shape is K T & K at their best!

K T & K "Bluebird and Apple Blossom Set" on "America" shape as pictured in the 1923-24 Montgomery Ward Catalog. The covered butter, again the most expensive piece, was $1.35. Note this is the same exclusive K T & K decal as appears on the "Bluebird of Happiness" dinnerware above.

Early eagle and circle, mark #1. 1900-1915.

Mark #2, 1910-1920s, may have date or date code.

Early K T & K bluebird 7.5" jug and close-up of decal, mark #1, c. 1900. $250.

"Flying Blue Bird" covered casserole on "Niana" shape, mark #2, c. 1920. Fabulous condition. $250.

Four "Flying Blue Bird" platters on "Niana" shape, in three different sizes, mark #2, c. 1920. 14.5" platter, $150. 13" platter, $125. 10" platter, $100.

Amazing 7" hot water pitcher, from pitcher and bowl set, mark #2. $400.

Two creamer and sugar sets, "Niana" dinnerware shape, one on left with two inner rims. Creamers, $55. Sugars, $85.

5" jug with lid, "Niana" shape, $150. Jug also came in 4", $85. 6", $175. 7", $250.

Three 7.5" dinner plates, mark #2, $40 each.

Two slightly-different sized teapots, "Niana" shape, $250 each.

Two different styles of K T & K double egg cups, $40 each.

Early butter with cover, "Niana" shape, c. 1918. Fair condition, $75. In perfect condition, if available, $250.

Soup bowl, with inner blue rim, $40.

Deep bowl, $45.

Very unusual coffee mug
with saucer, $75.

Ramekin with ramekin plate, $40.

Sauce bowl with attached underplate with browning and crazing, $25.

Pieces from K T & K child's set. The child's tureen, $150. Child cups, $20 each. Serving bowl from child's set, $30.

Close up of the "Flying Blue Birds" decals.

Hard to find three pint pitcher in "Victory" shape with "Bluebirds and Apple Blossoms" decal. $250.

Two different sizes of platters in "Bluebirds in Apple Blossoms" pattern. Large platter, $85. Small platter, $60.

Covered butter in "Victory" shape, with "Bluebirds and Apple Blossoms" decal, c. 1922. $250.

Close up of "Bluebirds and Apple Blossoms" decal used exclusively by K T & K.

Creamer and sugar in "Victory" shape, "Bluebirds in Apple Blossoms" pattern, mark #2. Set, $150.

Two deep bowls in "Bluebirds in Apple Blossoms" pattern, slightly different decal placement. $55 each.

Three sizes plates in "Bluebirds in Apple Blossoms" pattern. Dinner plate, $30. medium plate, $25. small plate, $20.

Oval serving bowl in "Bluebirds in Apple Blossoms" pattern, $45.

Cup and saucer in "Bluebirds in Apple Blossoms" pattern, $40 set.

Bluebird decoration on "Traymore" shape, c. 1925. The "Traymore" shape was K T & K's attempt to copy Haviland's "Ransom." Plate, $40. Serving bowl, $55.

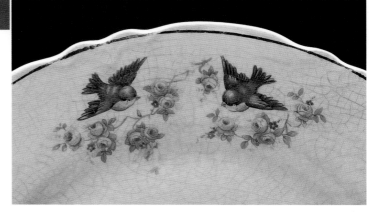

Covered casserole, "Bluebirds in Apple Blossoms" on "America" shape. $250.

A different K T & K bluebird treatment on cup, saucer, and dinner plate, mark #2. Cup and saucer, $30. Plate, $30.

K T & K medium platter, dated 1927, mark #2, $125.

K T & K plate with standard bluebird treatment, dated 1927. $35.

K T & K Deep bowl with standard bluebird decal, "Victory" shape, $75.

A large meat platter unknown shape or pattern name, marked K T & K, dated 1925, 17", very good condition, $200.

A child's tea set, attributed to K T & K by Mary Frank Gaston in *Collector's Encyclopedia of Knowles, Taylor and Knowles China* on page 108. No mark on this set. Small teapot, $75. Creamer, $30. Small plates, $25. Cup and saucer, $35. If the set were complete, the price would be in the $500 range.

A different bluebird treatment on "Victory" shape sauce boat. $40.

Homer Laughlin China Company

Homer Laughlin China Company began in 1873 in East Liverpool and moved to Newell, West Virginia, in 1929 where it continues to operate today as one of the largest china manufacturing companies in the world. Somehow Homer Laughlin Company managed to adapt and thrive through the depression, despite competition from less expensive foreign imports, wars, the changing tastes of the America consumer, labor problems, financial difficulties and more. Its continued prosperity is a tribute to its management and the artistry of the Homer Laughlin designers.

Homer Laughlin's "Empress" shape with bluebird decoration is probably the most available and popular of all bluebird treatments ever made. "Empress" dinnerware was introduced in 1914 and kept in production for many years according to Jo Cunningham and Darlene Nossman's *Homer Laughlin Guide to Shapes and Patterns.* Most "Empress" dinnerware with bluebird decals is dated in the 1920s.

The earliest bluebird decorations I've found on Homer Laughlin pieces are on the "Cable" shape, a lovely white ironstone produced in the 1900s. Collectors can also find bluebird decals on many other of Homer Laughlin's dinnerware shapes – the "Hudson" shape from the early 1900s, the "Kwaker" shape from the mid-1920s, the "Newell" shape of the late 1920s, the "Republic" shape throughout the 1920's, the "Riviera" shape of the mid-1930s, the "Tea Rose" shape from the 1930s and some shapes I haven't been able to identify.

Homer Laughlin "Empress"

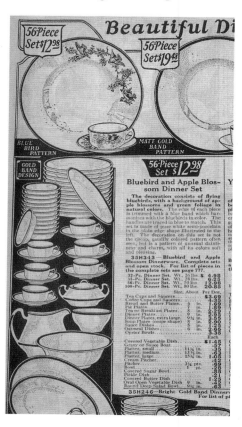

1927 Sears Roebuck Co. catalog ad for "Bluebird and Apple Blossom Dinner Set." Shapes are unmistakably Homer Laughlin "Empress." By this time, the price for a 32-piece set had increased to $4.95. A customer could special order service platters, pitchers, creamers, sugar bowls or the most expensive piece, a covered vegetable dish, which cost $1.45. Covered butter dishes were also an extravagance at $1.25.

Page from 1928-29 Chicago Mail Order Co. Catalog selling a "Bluebird Design" 32-piece set of Homer Laughlin "Empress" bluebird for $3.48.

Homer Laughlin "Empress" mark. Not all
"Empress" pieces are marked in this fashion.
Many are marked as shown below.

Homer Laughlin "Made in USA" mark with code.

No collection is ever complete without the elusive Homer
Laughlin "Empress" teapot, dated 1921. This one is perfect.
Courtesy of Stephanie and Tom Trambaugh. $800 or more.

Homer Laughlin "Empress" bluebird decal with blue edged rim.

The round "Empress" covered casserole, $225 and the oval
"Empress" covered casserole, $225.

Two sizes of Homer Laughlin "Empress" creamers. Individual creamer, $50. Regular creamer, $75.

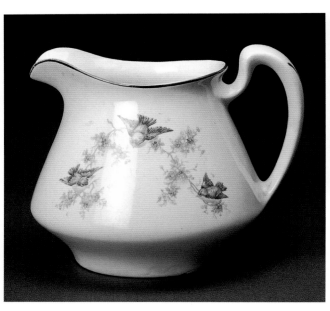

"Empress" shape jug or pitcher, $200.

Two "Empress" dinner plates, one with outer and inner blue rim. Single blue edge, $45. Inner and outer blue rim, $50.

"Empress" butter with cover, $250.

Large and small plate in "Empress" shape. Large plate, $45. Small plate, $25.

Large "Empress" meat platter, no blue edging at all, $110.

A set of six bone dishes. These recently sold for $730 on e-bay but a more reasonable price would be $400.

Four sizes of "Empress" platters. Meat platter, $110. Large platter, $100. Medium platter, $75. Small platter, $40.

"Empress" meat platter with K T & K style decal. Homer Laughlin was apparently always experimenting with different decals. Perhaps it is their open-mindedness and innovative thinking that has kept them successful. Meat platter, $75.

Unusual cake plate with tab handles on the side, inner blue rim. $125.

Part of Homer Laughlin's attention to detail is the placement of the one little bird on the inside of every cup. Cup and saucer, $85 set.

Oval serving bowl. *Courtesy of Joan Sloat, Now & Then Shoppe, Ft. Smith, Arkansas.* Serving bowl, $75.

Homer Laughlin deep bowl with, again, the trademark one little bird on the inside of the bowl. $75.

Some call this the "coffee mug," other refer to it as a "shaving mug," either way, $120. Possibly part of Homer Laughlin's 1900 Hotel Ware rather than "Empress."

Sauce boat with underplate with classic "Empress" lines. Sauce boat, $75. Underplate, $45.

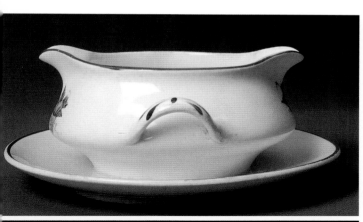

Gravy with attached underplate, beautiful from all angles, $350. *Courtesy of Stephanie and Tom Trambaugh.*

"Cable" shaped ironstone octagon covered jug, with lid, from early 1900s, $275.

Set of three custard bowls, no handles, marked Homer Laughlin "Empress." *Courtesy of Stephanie and Tom Trambaugh.* $75 each.

Unmarked but probably Homer Laughlin "Cable" jug, decorated with baby bluebirds, rimmed with gold, 9 1/2" tall, $250.

Homer Laughlin "Republic"

Homer Laughlin "Republic" mark, 1916-1960s.

Unmarked bread plate, probably Homer Laughlin "Republic" shape. $175.

"Republic" dinner plate. *Courtesy of Stephanie and Tom Trambaugh.* $45.

Homer Laughlin "Republic" cup and saucer, with little bird decal on inside of cup, $60 set.

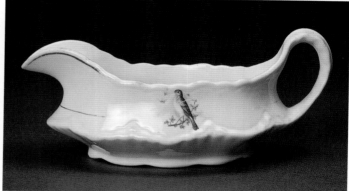

Sauce boat, marked Homer Laughlin "Republic," migrating birds in winter decal. $50.

Two "Republic" cups with decal shown at left. $25 each.

Three "Republic" bowls, $60 each, and mark on bowls.

"Republic" creamer, $75. Also came in individual size, $55.

Small serving bowl in "Republic" shape, $60.

Homer Laughlin "Hudson"

Homer Laughlin "Hudson" mark, introduced in 1908.

Three plates marked "Hudson." $25 each.

Wonderful "Hudson" covered casserole, $250.

Absolutely the ugliest piece of Homer Laughlin ever made! If it weren't marked, I wouldn't have believed this could have come out of the Homer Laughlin factory. It is heavy and thick, very low quality. Ugly "Hudson" platter, $20.

Homer Laughlin "Tea Rose"

"Tea Rose" shape, premium for Quaker Oats, c. 1937. Platter, $50.

Homer Laughlin "Newell"

Homer Laughlin's "Newell" was designed by Frederick Rhead who later created "Fiesta."

Mark typical of Homer Laughlin "Newell" shape from 1928.

Three "Newell" plates, $30 each.

Close up of "Newell" gadrooned edging and unusual decal with orange and blue flowers. This is the only bluebird decal on the "Newell" shape.

"Newell" cream pitcher, $55.

Small "Newell" bowl, $25.

Homer Laughlin "Kwaker"

Homer Laughlin "Kwaker" mark, c. 1924.

"Newell" tea cup, no saucer, little bird on inside, $20.

Medium "Newell" platter, 12", $35.

Very popular "Kwaker" shape creamer, $45.

Homer Laughlin Unidentified Pieces

Dated 1914, unidentified Homer Laughlin serving bowl with "dive bombing" bluebird decals, lots of gold trim, $35.

Unidentified Homer Laughlin platter with heavily embossed edges. Marked "Second Selection" perhaps because it was sold in an outlet for the pieces that did not meet quality control testing.

Limoges China Company
(American Limoges China Company)

Limoges China Company, a Sebring brothers of Sebring, Ohio, enterprise was in business from 1900 to 1955. The name changed to American Limoges China Company in the 1940s after legal problems with the City of Limoges, France. Not surprisingly, Limoges bluebird dinnerware looks very much like the bluebird produced by other Sebring brothers' ventures such as French China Company, Sebring Pottery Company, E. H. Sebring China Company, Saxon China Company, and Salem China Company. Aside from interesting twelve-sided and eight-sided shapes, Limoges bluebird dinnerware has very little to offer collectors of bluebird china. Most of it was probably manufactured to be given away as inexpensive premiums. Still, the creamers and sugar bowls are interesting for their designs and worthy of the price.

The Limoges China Company mark from the 1920s, the time period during which the company manufactured bluebird dinnerware.

Large and small Limoges dinnerware plates with gold outer rim and blue inner rim. Large plate, $35. Small plate, $25.

Close up of decal, inner blue rim and outer gold edging on Limoges bluebird dinnerware.

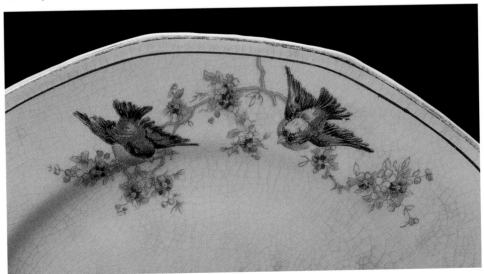

Pieces from twelve-sided dinnerware, interesting paneled effect. Saucers, $15 each. Small plate, without gold edging $20. Small bowl, with gold edging $30.

Eye-pleasing octagon shaped small plate, $45.

Eight-sided serving or underplate, $60.

This lovely six-sided sugar bowl with lid and elegant art-deco styling was part of the "Socialite" dinnerware pattern. $75.

Twelve-sided medium platter with baby bluebirds decal, $55.

D. E. McNicol Pottery

D. E. McNicol Pottery Company of East Liverpool, Ohio, and later, Clarksburg, West Virginia, operated from 1892-1960. D. E. McNicol is well known for its early calendar and commemorative plates that were usually personalized with the name of a local entrepreneur and given away as advertising and promotional pieces. Many of those specialty items were edged with bluebird decals. McNicol's designers apparently recognized early-on the great demand for china decorated with bluebirds. They experimented with many different bluebird treatments, any of which could show up on any of their dinnerware shapes. Collecting McNicol bluebird china can be fun. Even though some of the shapes and treatments are a little outlandish, the prices are not.

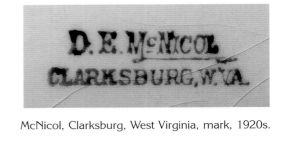

McNicol, Clarksburg, West Virginia, mark, 1920s.

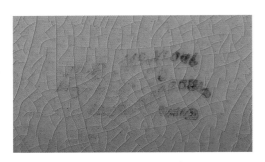

Early, c. 1905-1915, D. E. McNicol mark.

McNicol mark from 1915-1929.

1916 McNicol advertising plate, edged with bluebirds, center picture of wild ducks, $55. This may have been one of the earliest, if not the earliest calendar plate produced by McNicol.

Two McNicol advertising plates from 1921. One celebrating Armistice Day, $55, the other commemorating Christmas, 1920. $55.

15.5" x 11.5" large McNicol platter with gold rim, ten bluebirds, probably the "Ideal" shape, c. 1920. $150.

Bluebird decals on calendar plates.

"Ideal" shape, dinner plate with gold edging, c. 1920. $45.

Very graceful and dainty bluebird cup and saucer, "Ideal" shape, edged in gold trim, c. 1920. $70.

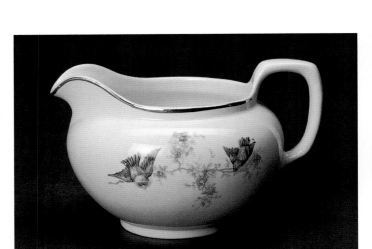

"Laurel" shape with a singing bluebird in cartouche decal, c. 1919. $150.

Jug in "Laurel" shape. This one is as perfect as the day it was made. $275. I'm still grieving over a teapot in this shape that slipped through my fingers. "Laurel" bluebird teapot, $400.

Same "Ideal" shape, different bluebird decal, c. 1920. $40.

Standard "McNicol" dinner plate with no edging or embossing. $45.

Over-the-top McNicol "Ohio" sugar bowl and lid, c. 1915. It doesn't get any more decorated than this. $150.

A curvaceous "Ohio" covered casserole with lid, c. 1915. $250.

A fabulous grouping of McNicol "Ohio" dinner plates. *Courtesy of Stephanie and Tom Trambaugh.* $55 each plate.

McNicol "Ohio" dinner plate, cup and saucer. *Courtesy of Stephanie and Tom Trambaugh.* Dinner plate, $55. Cup and saucer. $65.

T. A. McNicol Pottery Company

T. A. McNicol, following in his brother D. E.'s footsteps, opened a pottery company in East Liverpool in 1913. It closed in 1929. T. A. never found his niche, apparently, for there is not much china marked "T. A. McNicol" still around. That goes double for bluebird china. The one piece I've found is not remarkable.

T. A. McNicol mark from 1924.

An unremarkable T. A. McNicol creamer. $45.

Mercer Pottery

Mercer Pottery of Trenton, New Jersey, was a major player in the early American pottery business. The company was started early, in 1868, and lasted until the depression but unfortunately the trail has grown cold. Not much has been written about the wares produced by this great company. One thing is certain, however, there is very little Mercer bluebird china. I have only seen one piece, shown below.

Mercer Pottery Company mark that appears on bluebird china, c. 1890s.

This is it, the one piece of Mercer bluebird I've been able to find. It's made of a heavy ironstone pottery, heavy enough to be restaurant ware. Small plate, $40.

Mount Clemens Pottery

Mount Clemens Pottery started producing china in Mount Clemens, Michigan, in 1915. In 1920, S. S. Kresge Company acquired Mount Clemens and operated it as a subsidiary until 1965. Mount Clemens produced charming and attractive but simple bluebird dinnerware with several different decals. However, only the basic pieces, plates and bowls, seem to have surfaced. We haven't spotted a platter, creamer, sugar or even a cup and saucer, although there must be some out there somewhere. Prices are moderate.

Mount Clemens mark #1, c. 1920s.

Mount Clemens mark on its "Montel" dinnerware from 1920s.

Two Mount Clemens "Montel" plates, inner and outer blue rims, dated 1921. Large plate, $40. Small plate, $30.

Mount Clemens large and small dinner plates, outer rim only in blue, dated 1925. Large plate, $35. Small plate, $25.

Different bluebird plate on "Montel" shape, inner and outer blue rims, dated 1922, $30.

Mount Clemens bowl, dated 1926, plain edge. $40.

National China Company

The National China Company was formed in 1899 in East Liverpool, Ohio. The company moved to Salineville, Ohio, in 1911, where it was located until it went out of business in 1929. In 1918, National introduced its most popular line of dinnerware, "La Rosa," which was in production for many years and occasionally decorated with bluebirds. "La Rosa" bluebird is especially pleasing and appealing but priced on the high-end. Platters marked "National China Company" abound but are apparently not part of the "La Rosa" line. Other pieces are much harder to locate.

A large "National" platter with inner and outer blue rim, $125.

National mark, c. 1911-1925.

National "La Rosa" mark, 1918-1929.

National 13" platter and 11" platter edged with blue rim, both dated 1924. 13" platter, $80. 11" platter, $75.

Large, 15" National meat platter. *Courtesy of Stephanie and Tom Trambaugh.* $150.

11" platter, no rim, $75.

A 9.5" plate with peachy-breasted bluebirds, $50. A 9" inch plate with yellow-breasted bluebirds, $45.

National "La Rosa" cup and saucer, hard to locate, $55.

Gravy with attached underplate, $150.

A different bluebird treatment on 7" plate, $25.

Edward J. Owen China Company

The Edward J. Owen China Company existed in Minerva, Ohio, from 1902 to 1930. Surprisingly, this Company won the gold medal for the best domestic semi-porcelain at the Louisiana Purchase Exposition in St. Louis, Missouri, in 1904. (Where was K T & K when this prize was awarded?) It was probably not Owen's bluebird china that was entered into the competition. Owen bluebird dinnerware is plain and almost undecorated as if the designers wanted nothing – not even the pattern – distracting from the appreciation of their prize winning china. Owen bluebird china is moderately available and moderately priced.

Edward J. Owen China Company mark, touting their Gold Medal at the Louisiana Purchase Exposition in St. Louis.

Close-up of most commonly used bluebird decals.

A very creamy, smooth ivory china is the basis for Owen China Company's bluebird treatment, bowls, $35 each.

Owen's large platter, $75.

Grouping of Owen's bluebird cups and saucers, $40 each.

Owen's bluebird creamer in great condition. None of these pieces were overly fancy or overly decaled. $75.

Bowl with single, somber bird in flight, $30.

Another small bowl, one small bluebird decal, $30.

Pope-Gosser China Company

The Pope-Gosser China Company of Coshocton, Ohio, near East Liverpool, started production in 1903. The factory was closed in 1929, only to re-open in 1935 and close again in 1958. "Louvre" and "Edgemore" were their two most popular dinnerware lines c. 1915-1920 and both are available in bluebird patterns. "Louvre" is a fancy embossed dinnerware shape, imitative of Haviland's "Ransom" dinnerware and "Edgemore" is sleek, plain and unembossed with looped handles and knobs. While there's not a tremendous amount of Pope-Gosser bluebird, there is still plenty to go around. Moderately priced.

Pope-Gosser mark from 1920s, appears on all their bluebird dinnerware.

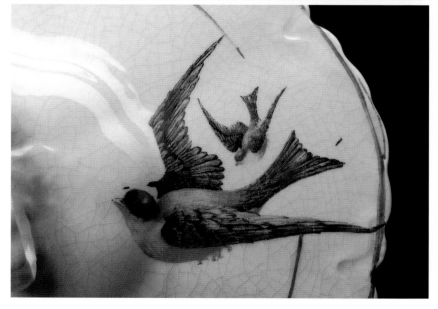

A covered dish from the Pope-Gosser "Louvre" dinner service. A collector's delight! Covered casserole with lid, $250.

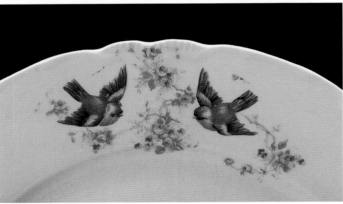

Pope-Gosser meat platter with familiar bluebird treatment, very well done, dated 1922. $185.

"Louvre" dinner plates with embossed design along the edges and baby bluebird decal, in never-used condition, $70 each.

Pope-Gosser meat platter, unusual bluebird treatment, c. 1915. $85.

The Potters' Co-Operative Company, Dresden Pottery

The Potters' Co-Operative Co., Dresden Pottery, was established in East Liverpool, Ohio, in 1876 and incorporated in 1882 according to a company brochure we located at the East Liverpool Museum of Ceramics. The company was gone – absorbed or dissolved – by 1925. The earliest bluebird treatment by The Potters' Co-Operative Company is dated 1920 and the latest probably produced around 1925. Four different marks can be found on their bluebird china, as shown below. The Company was capable of producing some excellent pieces of vitrified bluebird china but they were apparently not able to do it consistently. Most is only medium quality but nonetheless worthwhile for the interesting bluebird treatments.

Cover page from Potters' Co-operative Company brochure.
Courtesy of Museum of Ceramics, East Liverpool, Ohio.

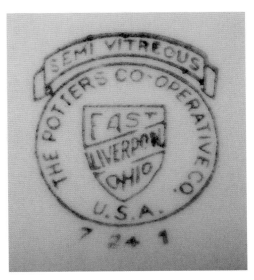

The Potters' Co-operative Company mark #2
c. 1920-1925.

The Potters' Co-operative Company mark #1,
c. 1920-1925.

Dresden China mark #3, c. 1908-1915.

The Potters' Co-operative Company, mark #4, c. 1915-1920.

The same uncommon bluebird decal, used exclusively by The Potters' Co-operative Company, appears on this large meat platter, $100.

An medium platter of excellent quality featuring another 1921 bluebird decal. $100.

Covered casserole with classic art deco styling, dated 1924. $250. One of my personal favorites.

A medium-quality covered casserole with uncommon bluebird treatment, dated 1920. $150.

A plate for baby with sweet baby bluebirds, c. 1920. $250.

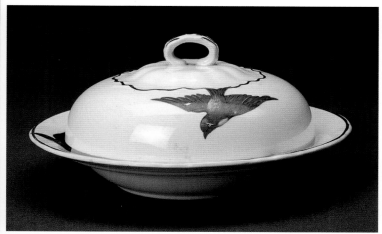

Butter with cover, matches oyster tureen below, c. 1915. $200.

A seldom-seen large oyster tureen, vitreous as opposed to semi-vitreous, fancy and gold-trimmed, c. 1915. $300.

Cups and saucers with "Dresden China" mark, c. 1915. Poor quality. $20 each.

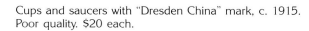

Salem China Company

The Salem China Company began operation in Salem, Ohio, in 1898, and was sold to F. A. Sebring in 1918. Salem closed its Ohio operation in 1967. Salem's bluebird china treatments and shapes are virtually indistinguishable from those produced at other Sebring companies such as French China Company, Sebring China Company, Saxon China Company and American Limoges China Company. Much of the dinnerware is twelve-sided and paneled. Because of the higher than average supply of Salem bluebird, prices are fairly low, except in cases of unusual pieces.

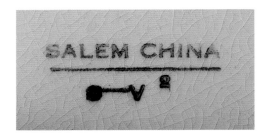

Salem China, mark #1, c. 1920.

Salem China, mark #3, c. 1918-1925.

Salem China, mark #2, c. 1920.

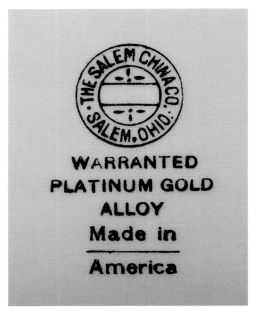

Salem China, mark #4, c. 1925-1930.

Twelve-sided dinner plate and serving bowl with familiar bluebird decal. Plate, $35. Serving bowl, $45.

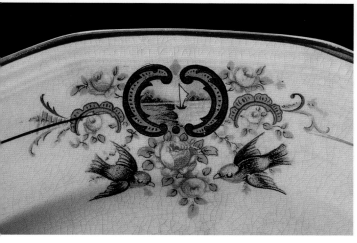

Twelve-sided dinner plate with a very involved bluebird decal consisting of a sailboat on a lake in a cartouche, surrounded by large pink roses in bloom with two little bluebirds completing the whole idyllic scene, mark #3. $30.

Charming twelve-sided serving platter. $50.

Dinner plate, cup and saucer with baby bluebird treatment. Plate, $35. Cup and saucer, $35.

Outstanding butter with cover by Salem, mark #1, c. 1920, in excellent condition, $250.

Magnificent bluebird in cartouche on ivory colored china, edged in silver, mark #4. Large Dinner plate, $45. Medium platter, $60. Small platter, $35.

Saxon China Company

The Saxon China Company, of Sebring, Ohio, has a history that is inextricably entwined with the various operations of the Sebring brothers and anything but completely clear. According to one source, the Saxon China Company was formed in 1911 and along with the French China Company and the Strong Manufacturing Company consolidated under the management of the Sebring Manufacturing Company in 1916. However, another source mentions a merger between the French China Company and the Saxon China Company in 1907, implying that Saxon existed as early as 1907. Under the Sebring umbrella, Saxon retained its separate existence until, along with French China Company, it vanished from the scene in 1932, according to one source. According to another, its demise came in 1929. Quite an amazing bit of confusion for such a prominent and well connected company. In 1934, the factory was reopened as the French-Saxon China Company and continued production until 1964.

Saxon China Company mark, c. 1900-1907.

S. C. Co. "Martha Washington" mark. c. 1926. Recall that Saxon's close relative, French China Co. had a Martha Washington mark as well.

Saxon China Company Shield mark, late 1920s.

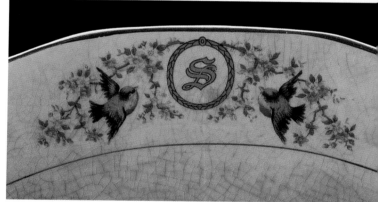

Medium platter, 12", with "S" monogram treatment. $35.

S. C. Co. "Martha Washington" twelve-sided plate with paneled outer edge and "Beady-eyed" decal. $35.

Large paneled edge platter, 13.5", with shield mark, unusual yellow breasted bird and lots of green in the foliage. Inner green ring and outer gold ring, c. 1925. $85.

Meat platter, 11.5", with traditional bluebird decal, twelve-sided with faint paneling. $75.

Meat platter, 15", with large bird and smaller following bird, twelve-sided and paneled. $125.

Small plates, 6.5", with beady eyed birds in flight decal and blue inner and outer rims. $35 each.

Four ruffled edge saucers with old mark and blue inner and outer rims. c. 1900-1907. $25.

Creamer with gold edge and traditional bluebird. $45.

E. H. Sebring China Company

E. H. Sebring China Company of Sebring, Ohio, c. 1909-1929, produced what was arguably the lowest-quality bluebird china ever made. It is thick, heavy and mottled with gray. A few bluebird decals were hastily applied, almost as an afterthought. E. H. S. bluebird has absolutely no appeal. In the event that your search turns up nothing but E. H. Sebring bluebird, keep looking.

Cup and saucer by E. H. Sebring, $20 set

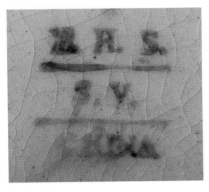

E. H. Sebring China Company mark, c. 1915-1920.

Medium E. H. Sebring bowl, $20. Small E. H. Sebring bowl, $10.

With better quality china, this could have been a beautiful piece. EHS gravy, $20.

Small platter or underplate with the twelve-sided effect used by all Sebring, Ohio, potteries. $20.

Close-up of typical careless EHS decal application.

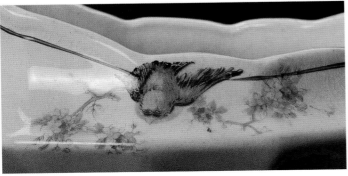

Sebring Pottery Company

The Sebring Pottery Company (c. 1887-1940) was owned by another of the Sebring brothers, F. A. Sebring. Founded in East Liverpool, the Company eventually moved to the town created by the Sebring brothers in 1898, Sebring, Ohio. Sebring's bluebird china is much like the bluebird dinnerware of other Sebring brother pot-teries but maybe on a slightly higher grade of china. The angled, paneled and tailored pieces from the early 1920's epitomize high-style of that era. The quality serving pieces appear infrequently. Ordinary pieces are readily available. Prices for Sebring Pottery Company pieces range from moderate to high.

Mark of Sebring Pottery Company, c. 1914-1930. Date appears under the mark beginning in 1919.

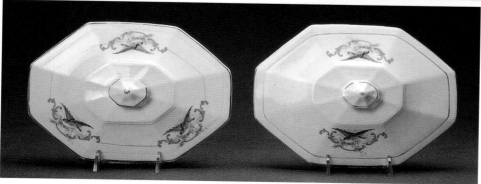

Two Sebring Pottery Company covered casseroles, slightly different decal placements, both dated 1921. $200 each.

This decal is used frequently on Sebring, Salem and Colonial Sterling.

Pair of Sebring cups and saucers, dated 1924, art deco embossing. $45 each.

Sebring covered casserole with standard bluebird treatment. $250.

Sebring dinner plate, dated 1924. $40.

13.5" platter, $85. 10.5" platter, $75. Both dated 1921 with gold edging.

This twelve-sided Sebring platter has very little bluebird decoration and an inside blue edge, dated 1922. $85.

Large creamer and sugar, dated 1921. Wonderful styling! Creamer, $80. Sugar bowl with lid, $125.

Small teapot with complicated shape, dated 1921. Very popular. $350.

Gravy with six-sided shape. $75.

Smith-Phillips China Company

Smith-Phillips China Company operated from 1901 to 1929 in East Liverpool, Ohio. The Company produced a limited amount of nice quality semi-porcelain dinnerware as well as hotel ware. Most of Smith-Phillips dinnerware is on fancy embossed shapes, rimmed with gold and heavily decorated. However, the only bluebird treatments we've found, while well-executed, appear on plain, simple shapes and only on the most basic pieces.

Smith-Phillips mark #1, c. 1901-1923.

Smith-Phillips mark #2, "Made in USA" has been added, c. 1915-1920s.

Platter, 13.5", dated 1917. $125.

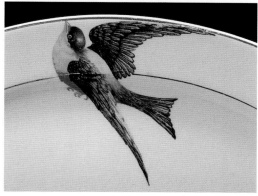

Smith-Phillips dinner plate, dated 1918, with single large bluebird treatment, $60.

Smith-Phillips 9.5" serving bowl, dated 1922, $75. 11.5" small platter, dated 1922. $75.

Steubenville Pottery Company

Steubenville Pottery Company of Steubenville, Ohio, was one of the grand old pottery companies in American history. The company was organized early, in 1879, and managed to make it until the 1950s, producing some classic American dinner lines along the way. They are probably best known for "American Modern" designed by Russell Wright and sold in the 1940s. Beginning about 1915 and on into the early 1920s, Steubenville released some beautiful bluebird dinnerware using a variety of colorful decals on a high grade of creamy white china. A bluebird motif also decorated a dinnerware from the 1930s, "Steubenville Ivory." Steubenville's efforts to produce a higher than average quality dinnerware kept them going for many years after much of their competition had succumbed to the pressures of foreign imports. Their bluebird china is a fine example of their efforts.

The Steubenville Pottery mark on most bluebird china, c. 1910-1920.

15.5" Steubenville Meat platter, c. 1920. $180.

Steubenville round covered casserole with soft bluebirds decal, c. 1920.

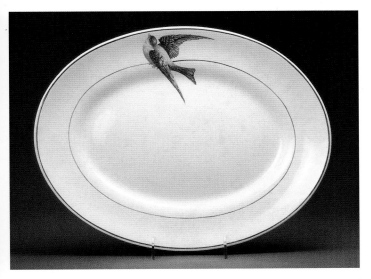

15" Steubenville Meat platter with single bluebird in flight decal, c. 1915. $175.

Steubenville Ivory mark from early 1930s.

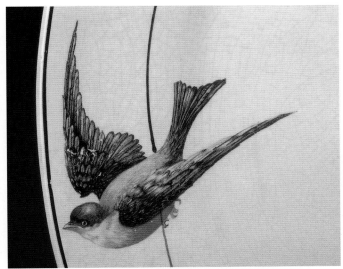

Closeup of Steubenville single bluebird in flight decal.

10" plate with bluebird in cartouche decal, c. 1920. $40.

Steubenville Ivory dinnerware with bluebird and butterflies motif on ivory background, c. 1930. Creamer, $25. Sugar with lid, $35. Gravy, $25.

Summit China Company

Summit China Company, organized in Akron, Ohio, in 1890, opened a second plant in Cleveland, Ohio, in about 1917 and closed sometime around 1930. Their bluebird children's tea set with the "Cleve-Ron" mark is the ultimate bluebird china collectible.

Creamer and sugar from children's tea set. Note that the children's pieces appear to be made to different scales. Creamer, $100. Sugar with lid, $150.

Summit China mark on children's bluebird set. Name comes from a combination of Summit's two locations, Cleveland and Akron. This mark was first used in 1917.

Cup, saucer and dinner plate from Summit China children's tea set, dated 1919. Plate, $50. Cup and saucer, $75.

A near-complete children's tea set by Summit China, dated 1919. Includes teapot with lid, creamer, sugar, four plates and four cups/saucers. This particular set is missing one saucer. If complete, $1,100 to $1,250.

The amazing little teapot from the Summit China children's tea set, c. 1919. Teapot only, $275.

This plate is marked "Summit China" in a circle. The mark was so faint it did not photograph. Neither Debolt nor Lehner show this Summit China mark so the plate and the mark remain somewhat of a mystery. Decorative plate, $125.

Taylor, Smith & Taylor

Taylor, Smith & Taylor produced some of the most outstanding china ever made in East Liverpool, Ohio. From their beginning in 1901 to the time they sold to Anchor Hocking Corporation in 1972, the company never settled for mediocrity. Their bluebird china treatment is breathtaking! The china is pearly white and smooth, the bluebird decals are artistically applied and colorful and the shapes are always elegant. It doesn't get any better than Taylor, Smith & Taylor "IONA" bluebird! However, expect to pay top dollar for it.

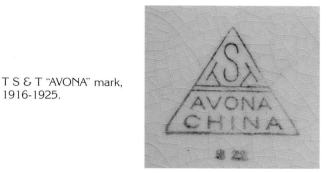

T S & T "AVONA" mark, 1916-1925.

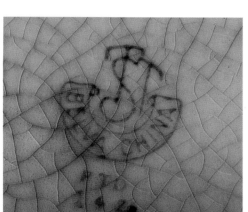

T S & T "BELVA" shape mark. 1920s only.

T S & T "BELVA" bluebird sugar bowl with lid, unfortunately very badly broken and repaired. Sugar bowl, if in perfect condition, $100.

Medium platter with "AVONA" mark and close up of an unusual T S & T bluebird treatment, $150.

T S & T "IONA" 6" plate, $85.

T S & T "IONA" mark, c. 1919-1927.

T S & T "IONA" covered casserole in mint condition, $350.

Set of four splendid T S & T "IONA" cups and saucers, $100 each.

Close-up of T S & T standard bluebird decal. Considered by some to be the best of all bluebird treatments.

Four T S & T "IONA" plates with uncommon bluebird treatment used frequently by T S & T. $65 each.

"IONA" Gravy with unusual bluebird treatment, $100.

Covered sugar in "IONA" shape, $100.

"IONA" platter with decal most commonly used by C. C. Thompson. Excellent condition, $225.

C. C. Thompson Pottery Company

C. C. Thompson Pottery Company of East Liverpool, Ohio, operated from 1889 to 1938. After World War I, the company dedicated its production entirely to the manufacture of semi-porcelain dinner ware, some of which was decorated with bluebirds. The pattern shapes are almost always stamped on the back of the piece along with the C. C. Thompson mark. Thus we know that Thompson used a bluebird treatment on their "Glenwood," "Francis," "Aladdin," "Chatham," and "Madison" shapes. Thompson's bluebird was only medium quality and most has crazed and turned brown over time.

Thompson "Aladdin" mark, c. 1905-1930.

Thompson "Francis" mark, 1905-1930.

Thompson "Chatham" mark, c. 1930

Thompson "Glenwood" mark, c. 1905-1930.

Thompson "Madison" mark, 1920s.

Thompson "Glenwood" cup and saucer, c. 1920. $45.

Unusual coffee mug, "Aladdin" shape, c. 1920. $75.

Three different sizes of Thompson "Glenwood" platters. Large platter, $150. Medium platter, $110. Small platter, $75.

Large meat platter, "Glenwood" mark, c. 1920. $150.

Double-egg cup, unmarked, attributed to Thompson, $110.

Thompson "Glenwood" gravy, $65.

Six piece grouping of Thompson "Glenwood" dinnerware. Large plate, $40. Small plate, $30. Serving bowl, $50. Soup bowl, $40. Cup and saucer, $45.

No pattern names on these two early Thompson platters, both are very worn, $30 each.

Thompson "Madison" small plate, $40.

Thompson "Glenwood" creamer, $75.

Pair of Thompson "Madison" dinner plates, $45 each.

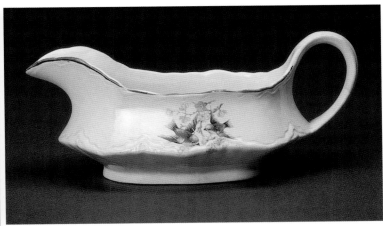

Thompson "Francis" gravy, $85.

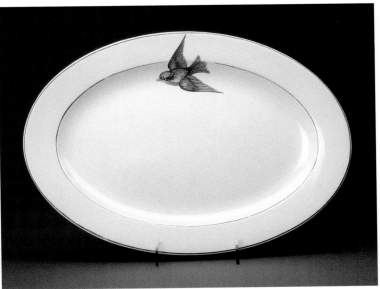

Large Thompson platter, no pattern name, c. 1920. $85.

Thompson "Chatham" plate, unusual decal, c. 1930. $25.

Two bluebird plates on "Francis" shape with heavy application of bluebird decals and gilded edges. $50 each. This was Thompson's version of Haviland's "Ransom" shape.

Vernon Kilns

Vernon Kilns of Vernon, California, (near Los Angeles) is well-known for its California pottery pieces produced in the 1930s to 1950s. However, what is not widely known, is that the company produced semi-porcelain fancy china dinnerware from 1916 to 1928. The name "Poxon China" appears on some of those earliest pieces. Vernon's bluebird china treatment is beyond scarce, it has nearly vanished from the American landscape.

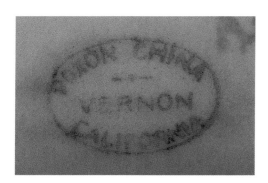

Vernon Kilns "Poxon China" mark, c. 1916.

Vernon "Poxon China" creamer, c. 1916. Fancy shape typical of the times. $175.

Another early Vernon China mark, c. 1920s.

Small ironstone platter marked "Vernon China" and dated 1926. $100.

Warwick China Company

Warwick China Company of Wheeling, West Virginia, began production in 1887 and closed its operation in 1951. During the 1920s while the bluebird dinnerware craze was at its peak, Warwick was making china primarily for hotels. We expected to find quite a bit of Warwick commercial-type china with one or more common bluebird treatments but a single restaurant dinner plate, pictured below, is the sum total our Warwick china finds.

Warwick China Company mark from 1920s.

Warwick China dinner plate with bluebird, c. 1920. $35.

Wellsville China Company

Wellsville China Company operated in Wellsville, Ohio, from 1900-1959 making semi-porcelain dinnerware and other related items. Wellsville became a subsidiary of Sterling China Company in 1959 and operated for another ten years, before it closed. During the 1920s, the Company produced a limited amount of tasteful and simple bluebird china. Platters in several sizes and dinner plates can be had, but beyond that, nothing else seems to be easily found.

Wellsville China Company mark from 1920s.

Wellsville China platter with standard bluebird decal, $150.

Wellsville China platter with baby bluebirds decal, $150.

West End Pottery

The West End Pottery of East Liverpool, Ohio, spanned a forty-five year period, from 1893 to 1938. Given that the company existed for so long, it is hard to explain why there is so little of their product available today. Finding actual West End Pottery bluebird china pieces to photograph has been difficult. Thus far, we've located one splendid West End Pottery platter in a collection and one rather ordinary dinner plate on e-bay. Fortunately for all collectors, the East Liverpool Museum of Ceramics maintains several of West End Pottery's original catalogs in their libraries and generously allowed us to photograph two different bluebird patterns we discovered in those catalogs.

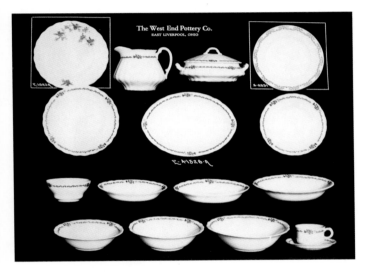

West End's bluebird pattern on "Seneca" shape. *Courtesy of Museum of Ceramics, East Liverpool, Ohio.*

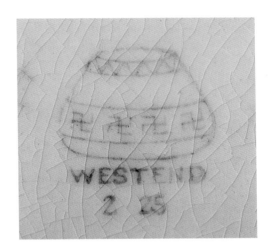

West End Pottery Company "Indian basket" mark, c. 1918-1928.

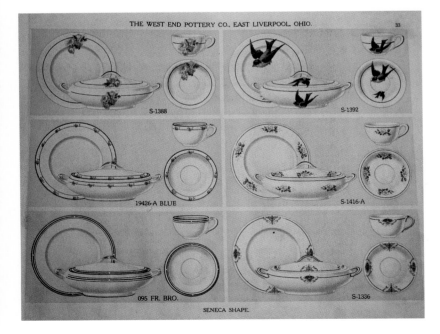

West End Pottery Company catalog page, showing bluebird china available on unidentified shape. *Courtesy of Museum of Ceramics, East Liverpool, Ohio.*

West End Pottery Company dinner plate with baby bluebirds, $40.

Large, 15", meat platter, c. 1920, $250. *Courtesy of Joan Sloat, Now & Then Shoppe, Ft. Smith, Arkansas.*

H. R. Wyllie China Company

H. R. Wyllie China Company of Huntington, West Virginia, c. 1905-1929, manufactured bluebird china almost from the date of its inception. Wyllie's early fancy shapes and heavy embossing make this bluebird a favorite with collectors. Much of it is well preserved and expensive.

H. R. Wyllie China Company mark, c. 1905-1920.

Two 6" one 8" bowl from fancy dinnerware set. 6" bowl, $60. 8" bowl, $80.

Small and medium H. R. Wyllie China Company platters, c. 1910. Close up of embossing on edges. Embossing "dresses up" the simple bluebird dinnerware, making it suitable for special occasions as well as for everyday use. Small platter, $125. Medium platter, $175.

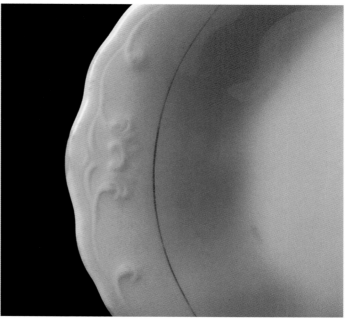

Two H. R. Wyllie China Company dinner plates and close-up of decal. $75 each.

A breathtaking large pitcher by H. R. Wyllie. This 8.5" pitcher with very fancy handle is in perfect, unused condition. Even the curved bottom edge is detailed with heavy embossing. $400.

Exceedingly rare Wyllie butter with cover, c. 1910. *Courtesy of Stephanie and Tom Trambaugh.* $400.

Cream pitcher with single realistic bluebird decal. Same fancy shape and embossing as on large pitcher. $150.

A much plainer bluebird pattern platter by H. R. Wyllie, c. 1920. $65.

Deep bowl, $100.

This little note glued to the back of an H. R. Wyllie saucer reads, "This was my mother's first set of dishes. They married 2/7/01."

Another bluebird treatment on a fancy Wyllie medium platter, c. 1910. $150.

Unknown and Unidentified

Butter Pats

Unmarked butter pat, #1. Gold edge and inner blue rim, $30.

Unmarked butter pat, #3. Bird is pointed west, outer blue edge, $30.

Unmarked butter pat, #2. Single bird at bottom of pat, outer blue rim. $30.

Unmarked butter pat, #4. Inner and outer blue rims, single central bird, $35.

Unmarked butter pat, #5. Embossed blue edging, realistic bird decal, $25.

Unmarked butter pat, #6. Plain edges, central single bluebird, $25.

Unmarked butter pat, #7. Twelve-sided butter pat with inner and outer blue rim. Baby bluebird decal, $35.

Unmarked butter pat, #8. Central single bluebird, inner blue circle, outer gold edge, $35.

Unmarked butter pat, #9. Dark blue inner and outer rim, realistic bluebird in flight. *Courtesy of Susan Wright.* $30.

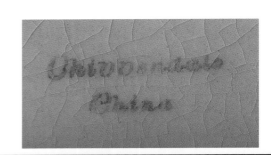

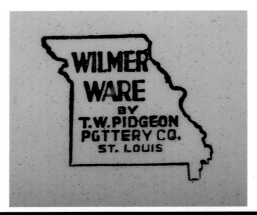

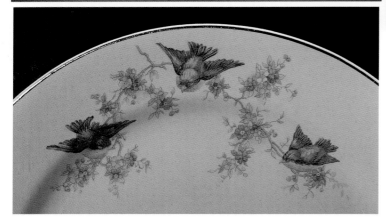

These cheaply made ironstone pieces are marked but the mark is indecipherable. Platter, $25. Creamer, $20. Gravy, $20.

Marked Wilmer Ware by T. W. Pidgeon Pottery Company, St. Louis, Missouri. Nothing is known about these pieces other than the information conveyed in the mark. The china is tan rather than white and edged in silver rather than gold. $30 each.

At best, these "El Capitan" plates are ordinary. Manufacturer remains a mystery. $20.

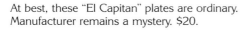

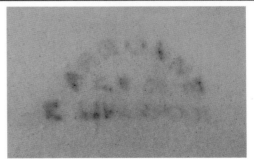

Gravy marked "Argonne East Liverpool", $35.

Marked "Buffalo Manufacturing Company" but not a product of Buffalo China Company as we had first believed. The bluebird treatment looks most like K T & K. However, Homer Laughlin also made the same platter at least once. Large warming dish with cover, $150. Small warming dish for child, $75.

Possible Oatmeal Premiums

Close up of decal and ribbed embossing which appears on the following unmarked pieces. These were most likely oatmeal premiums. They could have been made by K T & K, Homer Laughlin, Salem or some other less prominent manufacturer. Collectors can still complete a set of this charming pattern the way their grandmothers did, one piece at a time.

Unmarked cup and saucer, $50.

Unmarked creamer, interesting shape and ribbed bottom, $75.

Unmarked deep bowl, $50.

Unmarked gravy, $100.

Unmarked octagonal serving bowl, $100.

Unmarked round serving bowl, $75.

Unmarked octagonal serving platter, $100.

Unmarked But Not Un-Collectible

Unmarked pair of handled custard cups. Very well executed with a high degree of embossing. The single bluebird on the inside of the cup is characteristic of Homer Laughlin and Taylor Smith Taylor. However, these could easily be part of W. G. George's "Radisson" treatment.

Pair of unmarked high-quality double egg cups. *Courtesy of Susan Wright.* $100 each.

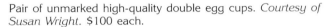

Large unmarked salad bowl with decal used commonly by Owen of Minerva, Ohio. *Courtesy of Susan Wright.* $150.

Pair of large unmarked 10" sauce boats. These look to be from the early 1900s and could be part of K T & K's hotel ware. They also look like they might have been made by Homer Laughlin. However, they could have been done by any of the early East Liverpool potteries. $125 each.

Unmarked luster-edged bluebird platter, probably Homer Laughlin, $100.

Unmarked 12.5" vase. *Courtesy of Joan Sloat, Now &
Then Shoppe, Ft. Smith, Arkansas.* No marks. $150.

Cream pitcher with great little shape. No mark but might be an
Edwin Knowles product. $100

Two unmarked coffee mugs. Heavy enough to be
restaurant ware. $80 each.

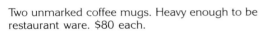

Unmarked plates from snack set. Crisp and bright decals. Could be
K T & K. $75 each plate.

Rare 4" coffee mug, unmarked, baby bluebirds decal. $100.

Shaving mug with curious little handle, unmarked, $85.

Advertising plate from Glazers Variety Store, Hancock Maryland. Commercial weight, unmarked. $55.

Covered casserole, unmarked, $175.

Partial set of children's dishes. Teapot, sugar bowl, three plates, three cups and saucers. $375, incomplete. Unable to track down the manufacturer of this distinctive shape.

Early, ornate cream pitcher. A-1 is stenciled in gold on the top front edge. $150.

Unmarked covered casserole. *Courtesy of Stephanie and Tom Trambaugh.* $175.

Unmarked 7" water pitcher. Early 1900s shape. *Courtesy of Stephanie and Tom Trambaugh.* $300.

Single bird, flying east on heavily embossed bowl with scalloped edges. No marks. No guesses. $25.

Beautiful creamy white and dark bluebirds 13.5" serving bowl, possibly made by Colonial, Saxon or Warwick. $150.

Close up of decal on unidentified pieces shown at right.

Unmarked cereal bowl, $50.

Three different sizes of plates, $60, $40 and $35 respectively.

Serving bowl with interesting shape, $80.

Small bowl, $35.

Platter with interesting shape, similar to Carrollton's shape. $80.

Bibliography

Altman, Violet and Seymour. *The Book of Buffalo Pottery*. Atglen, Pennsylvania: Schiffer Publishing Ltd., 1969.

Ayars, Walter. *Larkin China*. Summerdale, Pennsylvania: Echo Publishing, 1990.

Bagdade, Susan and Al. *Warman's American Pottery & Porcelain*. Iola, Wisconsin: Krause Publications, 2000.

Board of Trade, City of Trenton, N. J. *Industrial Trenton and Vicinity*. Wilmington, Delaware: George A. Wolf, 1900.

Colbert, Neva W. *Harker Pottery*. Paducah, Kentucky: Collector Books, 1993.

Cunningham, Jo. *American Dinnerware*. Paducah, Kentucky: Collector Books, 1982.

Cunningham, Jo. *Homer Laughlin A Giant Among Dishes*. Atglen, Pennsylvania: Schiffer Publishing Ltd., 1998.

Cunningham, Jo. *The Best of Collectible Dinnerware*. Atglen, Pennsylvania: Schiffer Publishing Ltd., 1999.

Cunningham, Jo and Nossaman, Darlene. *Homer Laughlin China Guide to Shapes and Patterns*. Atglen, Pennsylvania: Schiffer Publishing Ltd., 2002.

Debolt, C. Gerald. *Debolt's Dictionary of American Pottery Marks*. Paducah, Kentucky: Collector Books, 1994.

Gaston, Mary Frank. *Knowles, Taylor & Knowles China*. Paducah, Kentucky: Collector Books, 1996.

Jasper, Joanne. *American Dinnerware 1880s to 1920s*. Paducah, Kentucky: Collector Books, 1996.

Kovel, Ralph and Terry. *Kovel's New Dictionary of Marks*. New York, New York: Crown Publishers, Inc., 1986.

Lehner, Lois. *U. S. Marks on Pottery, Porcelain & Clay*. Paducah, Kentucky: Collector Books, 1988.

Limoges, Raymonde. *American Limoges*. Paducah, Kentucky: Collector Books, 1996.